The President, the Budget, and Congress

Other Titles in This Series

Westview Special Studies in Public Policy and Public Systems Management

The President, the Budget, and Congress: Impoundment and the 1974 Budget Act
James P. Pfiffner

There has always been a dispute over the power to spend federal funds, a power divided in the Constitution between Congress and the president. It was not until the Nixon administration, however, that the conflict erupted into a constitutional crisis. At the heart of the controversy was President Nixon's claim that he had the constitutional authority to refuse to spend funds that Congress had allocated. Reacting to what seemed to be a usurpation of congressional prerogatives, the judiciary became involved in the budgetary process for the first time: in a series of cases culminating in the Supreme Court, judges ordered that the impounded funds be released. To reassert its power vis-à-vis the "imperial presidency," Congress passed the 1974 Budget and Impoundment Control Act, limiting impoundment and reforming the traditional budgetary process.

This book is a comprehensive analysis of the controversy over presidential impoundment of funds. Professor Pfiffner covers fully the executive, legislative, and judicial roles in the controversy and concludes that impoundment was a major factor in the passage of the 1974 Budget Act.

James P. Pfiffner is assistant professor of political science at California State University at Fullerton.

The President, the Budget, and Congress: Impoundment and the 1974 Budget Act

James P. Pfiffner

Westview Press / Boulder, Colorado

Westview Special Studies
in Public Policy and Public Systems Management

Copyright © 1979 by Westview Press, Inc.

Published in 1979 in the United States of America by
Westview Press, Inc.
5500 Central Avenue
Boulder, Colorado 80301
Frederick A. Praeger, Publisher

HJ
2052
P52
1979

Library of Congress Cataloging in Publication Data
Pfiffner, James P.
The President, the budget, and Congress.
(Westview special studies in public policy and public systems management)
Includes index.
1. Executive impoundment of appropriated funds—United States. 2. United States—Appropriations and expenditures. 3. Budget—United States. I. Title.
HJ2052.P52   343'.73'034   79-552
ISBN: 0-89158-468-4
ISBN: 0-89158-495-1 pbk.

Printed and bound in the United States of America

To
BOOTH FOWLER
and
MARK CATES

two teachers who made a difference

Contents

Acknowledgments

Most of the research for this study was done while I was a research fellow at the Brookings Institution. I am grateful to Brookings for providing me with support and a congenial atmosphere within which to do research. Not the least of the benefits of working at Brookings is the stimulating group of scholars in residence. I am indebted to my friends and colleagues there who read earlier versions of this study and were so generous with their time and counsel. Among them are: Joel Aberbach, Ted Anagnason, Peggy Cuciti, Martha Derthick, Dan Fiorino, Scott Harris, Bob Hartman, Hugh Heclo, Stephen Hess, Herb Kaufman, Dan Metlay, Richard Nathan, Gary Orfield, Gil Steiner, and James Sundquist. I am also indebted to Austin Ranney for the amount of time he spent guiding, commenting upon, and criticizing my efforts. I would like to thank Clem Bezold and Jon Mills of the Center for Governmental Responsibility at the University of Florida at Gainesville for their help and for the use of the center's files on impoundment. I am also grateful to other colleagues and friends who read and commented on portions of my manuscript or allowed me to use their written materials: David Adamany, Chuck Adrian, Larry Baum, Don Brown, Bob Dickens, George Edwards, John Ellwood, David Fellman, Joel Grossman, Joel Havemann, Deb Hoeflin, Pat McInturff, Max Neiman, and Jim Thurber. Special thanks are due to Lou Fisher, the foremost expert on presidential impoundment of funds, who went over an earlier version of this manuscript with a fine-toothed comb and saved me from many embarrassments.

Mistakes or inaccuracies that remain in the manuscript certainly cannot be blamed on the above fine group of scholars. Although it is customary for authors to accept the entire blame for errors themselves, I prefer to believe that any remaining inaccuracies are due to the tiny gremlins who continually hound serious scholars.

J.P.P.

1
Introduction

The year 1974 marked a turning point in American government. President Richard Nixon resigned his office under threat of impeachment by the House of Representatives. The Congress passed the Congressional Budget and Impoundment Control Act of 1974; the previous year it had passed the War Powers Resolution over a presidential veto. The Supreme Court limited the doctrine of executive privilege in *U.S.* v. *Nixon* and ruled against the administration's claim to the power to impound congressionally provided funds.

Congress and the president battled over policy priorities and institutional prerogatives. The Constitution had established a system in which governmental power is divided among three branches, each having a specific set of powers and prerogatives. The relative power of Congress, the presidency, and the federal courts in the forming of governmental policy, however, has fluctuated over the past two centuries, the executive branch becoming predominant in the twentieth century. During the second term of Richard Nixon's presidency, Congress had begun to reassert its waning constitutional prerogatives, and the conflict took on the air of a constitutional crisis.

At issue were the reins of power and the substance of policy. Republican President Nixon and the Democrat-controlled Congress were vying for control of the direction of public policy, possession of the purse strings being a central element. This book will examine the clash between the two branches of government over fiscal power, a clash that resulted in the most important reform of the federal budgetary process since the

Budget and Accounting Act of 1921. Congressional initiative and reaction to the presidency on other issues will be examined to provide a context, but the purpose of the book is to explain the constitutional changes in the budgetary process taking place at mid-twentieth century.

When the constitutional balance between the president and Congress shifts, two dynamics are involved: partisan political conflict and assertion of institutional prerogative, which may cut across party lines. Both factors played an important role in the struggle over control of the budgetary process. As a result of the clash with President Nixon over the power of the purse, and buttressed by the legitimacy provided by the federal courts, Congress in 1974 passed the Congressional Budget and Impoundment Control Act.

The attempt by Congress to regain control of spending power through the 1974 Budget Act was the result of several factors. At the surface there was an overt clash of policy priorities between a relatively conservative Republican, Richard Nixon, and a Congress controlled by Democrats. Relying on what he said was a mandate from the voters in the 1968 and 1972 elections, President Nixon attempted to change fiscal priorities from the expansive domestic spending of Lyndon Johnson's War on Poverty to a greater emphasis on defense and foreign policy, by cutting the social programs. The Democrats who controlled Congress were not sanguine about his initiatives. These conflicting policy preferences between the incumbents of the two institutions could be expected to produce political friction.

Over and above the partisan differences, President Nixon was confrontational when he dealt with the Congress. In part this may have been a shift in strategy from his early days in the White House when he was frustrated in his attempts to get legislative initiatives through the House and Senate. In the words of one scholar he decided to *"take over* the bureaucracy and *take on* the Congress."[1] One aspect of this style was his assertion that, as president, he had the constitutional power to impound funds appropriated by Congress. This was in marked contrast to Lyndon Johnson's method of flexibly soft-pedaling his impoundments. In addition to conflicts over fiscal priorities, President Nixon's confrontational style was also exhibited in his "stonewalling" of Congress and the courts in their attempts to obtain tapes and other information relevant to the impeachment inquiry.

The factors of partisan differences and style are difficult to distinguish from matters of institutional prerogative and constitutional right. This is, nevertheless, an important distinction to make. It is this book's contention that the 1974 Budget Act would not have been passed were it not for a threat perceived by the Congress that its constitutional spending power was being usurped by President Nixon. This threat was characterized by the growth of the "imperial presidency," the increasing domination of the budgetary process by the institutionalized presidency, and the radical escalation in the use of impoundment to alter congressional spending priorities.

The idea of the imperial presidency reflects a change in perspective on the benevolence of presidential power.[2] The twentieth century has seen a drastic increase in the size and expansion of the functions of the national government in the United States. In the process of dealing with the Great Depression, World War II, and the cold war, the size of the government grew and with it the power of the executive branch. The presidency also became increasingly involved in the domestic areas of civil rights and growing urban unrest. During these years the presidency enjoyed widespread support for initiatives meant to deal with these problems.

One of the main factors in the changing perception of this aggregation of power in the presidency was the gradual disenchantment of the public with the war in Vietnam. Members of Congress, many of them liberals, began to look upon presidential government with increasing distrust. This attitude reached its greatest intensity during the administration of Richard Nixon, although he was in fact continuing a trend that had begun in the 1930s. He did, however, depart from precedent in important ways in his conduct of the presidency.

One aspect of the imperial presidency is the use of actions of questionable legality to pursue political goals. For example, President Nixon attempted to dismantle the Office of Economic Opportunity before its legislative mandate had expired, an action that was reversed by the courts. Another example is his unprecedented attempt to use the pocket veto during a five-day Christmas recess rather than at the end of a session of Congress. There was also considerable criticism from both sides of the aisle of the secret bombing of Cambodia.

More germane to the present argument about the threat to the congressional spending power are the domination of the budgetary process by the presidency and the use of impoundment by President Nixon. The modern budgetary process was established with the passage of the Budget and Accounting Act of 1921, which set up an executive budget and created the Bureau of the Budget. Since then, presidents have used the technique of central legislative clearance, exercised through the Budget Bureau, to gain increasingly centralized control over the whole governmental bureaucracy as well as control over spending priorities. An important attempt at presidential control was the creation of the Office of Management and Budget by President Nixon in 1970.

The greatest impetus for the 1974 budget reform was President Nixon's impoundment of funds, that is, his refusal to spend money appropriated by Congress. Previous presidents had impounded funds but not to the extent or in the manner that President Nixon did. Particularly annoying to the Congress was his refusal to spend water pollution control funds that had been provided in legislation passed over a presidential veto. His action amounted to an absolute veto. He also impounded funds that had been provided in existing legislation by not including them in his budget request for the following fiscal year. This permitted the president's proposed budget to take precedence over existing law. An important, though symbolic, act was his declaration that, as president, he had the constitutional right to impound funds. The impoundment controversy became so heated that members of Congress spoke of a constitutional crisis, and the Judiciary Committee of the House seriously considered using the impoundment issue as one of the grounds for impeachment.[3] Thus did the 1974 budget reform grow out of a perceived threat to the congressional spending power.

Aside from settling a few claims against the treasury, the

judiciary has traditionally stayed out of the budgetary process. This has a sound basis in the functional separation of powers; the courts have little expertise in the administrative aspects of public policy, and they have little legitimate mandate to make decisions about fiscal policy. In addition, the Supreme Court has shied away from "political questions," that is, matters constitutionally delegated to another branch or hotly contested issues calling for a political resolution. Yet in 1971 district courts began to accept cases challenging the president's impoundment power, and in 1975 the Supreme Court ruled against the president's argument that he could legally withhold congressionally provided funds.

The courts accepted impoundment cases for a variety of reasons, one of them being the failure of Congress to act quickly against impoundment. This resulted in an increasing number of litigants who claimed legal right to the withheld funds. Another reason was the role the judiciary has sometimes played as interpreter of the Constitution and arbiter between the other two branches. Impoundment was an instance of the president and Congress directly disagreeing about an important statutory and constitutional question.

In addition, the courts may have accepted the cases because of the clarity of the legal issues involved. Although many of the legal questions concerned were complex, there was surprising unanimity on the part of the courts. In virtually all of the impoundment cases considered by courts at the district, circuit, and Supreme Court level, judges refused to uphold the government's contention that the president had the right to impound funds. Such a consensus among judges in widely varying jurisdictions is highly unusual. This adds weight to the conclusion that more than partisan politics was involved in the congressional reassertion of power in the 1974 Budget Act.

In addition to the external impetus to its action, there was also a felt need in the Congress to put its own house in order. The congressional budgetary process was sorely in need of revision. Revenue and expenditure bills were considered by different committees at different times with no institutional link between the two. Appropriations were passed in thirteen separate bills and the total budget was the sum of these separate acts, with no point in the process at which an overall view was taken.

What precipitated the formulation of the 1974 Budget Act was a proposal by President Nixon in July 1972 that he be given the authority to hold federal spending in fiscal 1973 to $250 billion. The House acceded, but the Senate refused to pass the necessary legislation, although it recognized the necessity of imposing some sort of discipline on congressional spending. Consequently, a joint committee was established to propose appropriate reforms of the congressional budgetary process.

The proposals of the joint committee that were finally adopted in the 1974 Budget Act set up a new timetable for the budgetary process. Budget committees were established in the House and Senate to consider the president's budget proposals as a whole and to propose initial spending targets and revenue levels reflecting congressional priorities. The targets would be adopted in the beginning of the process and appropriations bills would be subject to the ceilings subsequently set in the concurrent resolutions. Total revenue and expenditures would be considered together and choices would have to be made explicitly among competing policy priorities.

Title X of the 1974 act confronts the impoundment problem. Under its provisions, if the president wants to withhold funds for a short while, he must inform the Congress; his proposal is subject to a veto by either house. If he wants to rescind the money completely, he must receive the positive approval of both houses. These impoundment control provisions originated as a compromise between House and Senate versions of previously proposed antiimpoundment legislation. The new measure was meant to balance the need for some administrative discretion in spending while at the same time protecting congressional prerogatives.

Chapter 2 of this book begins the analysis of constitutional change in the budgetary process by considering the development of executive domination of the budgetary process. The sharing of powers between Congress and the president, with their differing constituencies and terms of office, was meant to ensure a certain amount of rivalry between them. The budgetary arena is one in which they both share power, and it has traditionally been a source of friction between the two branches.

Since the practice of impoundment was so important to the congressional reassertion of the power of the purse, three chapters will deal with various aspects of it. Chapter 3 explains the technique itself and its use by various presidents. The legal justifications for impoundment by these presidents are critically analyzed in Chapter 4. Chapter 5 considers the litigation surrounding the impoundment controversy.

The political context of the controversy is set forth in Chapter 6, which examines other areas of confrontation between the president and Congress as well as previous attempts at budget reform. The culmination of the struggle was the Congressional Budget and Impoundment Control Act of 1974, which is the subject of Chapter 7. The reformed congressional budget process is explained, and the compromises built into the final version are analyzed. The conclusion, Chapter 8, examines the timing of the act and the attempt to disentangle partisan political factors from institutional issues in the passage of the act.

Notes

1. Richard Nathan, *The Plot that Failed* (New York: John Wiley, 1975), p. 8.

2. See Arthur M. Schlesinger, Jr., *The Imperial Presidency* (New York: Popular Library, 1974); and Thomas E. Cronin, "The Textbook Presidency and Political Science," in U.S., Congress, Senate, *Congressional Records*, 91st Cong., 2d sess., 1970, 116, 517102-15. I am using the term "imperial presidency" loosely, to denote the growing power of the presidency relative to the other two branches.

3. U.S., Congress, House, Committee on the Judiciary, *Statement of Information*, Book 12, *Impoundment of Funds*, Impeachment Hearings, 93rd Cong., 2d sess., May-June 1974.

2
The Development
of Executive Domination
of the Budgetary Process

In *The Federalist,* Madison describes fiscal power as "the most complete and effectual weapon with which any constitution can arm the immediate representatives of the people, for obtaining a redress of every grievance, and for carrying into effect every just and salutory measure."[1] The power of the purse may be the Congress' most complete and effectual weapon, but at mid-twentieth century the legislative branch was not dominant in fiscal matters. It was the institutionalized presidency that dominated the budgetary process, and in the early 1970s President Nixon used this power in unprecedented ways to pursue his policy goals.

This chapter explains how the Budget Bureau came to be the president's most important tool in centralizing his control over the budget. First it is necessary, however, to examine the spending power in the nineteenth century, for it was the lack of control over the budget near the turn of the century that spawned the movement toward the executive budget. The extent of presidential domination in 1974 makes sense only as the result of decades of increasing centralization of control located in the executive branch. The development of central legislative clearance will be considered from the 1920s to the 1960s. This will set the stage for the step-level increase in budget control asserted by President Nixon through the Office of Management and Budget and his impoundment practices. It is only in this context that it is possible to understand the congressional Budget and Impoundment Control Act of 1974.

The Spending Power in the Nineteenth Century

The early years of the budget of the United States were marked by a clash between the conflicting needs for fiscal control and administrative flexibility. The first appropriations act provided funds in very broad categories with $216,000 for the expenses of the civil list and $137,000 for the Department of War. The second and third appropriations acts (1790 and 1791) followed the same general categories, with both acts written on one page.[2] This reflected the ideas of Alexander Hamilton, who became secretary of the treasury in 1789. In accord with his advocacy of executive power, he favored the use of lump sum appropriations, giving discretion to the executive to spend funds where they were most needed.

The Jeffersonian Republicans, however, were wary of the growing power Hamilton wielded as secretary of the treasury, which they saw as a threat to the congressional spending power. Beginning in 1790 in an attempt to counter the executive, appropriations grew increasingly detailed.[3] In 1795 Hamilton resigned, and the House created a Committee on Ways and Means, which was renewed annually until it was made a standing committee in 1802. Albert Gallatin, a Jeffersonian, was on the Ways and Means Committee and led the move for more accountability to the Congress in spending. He introduced a series of amendments according to which appropriations could be "solely applied to the objects for which they are respectively appropriated."[4] In the late 1780s appropriations were becoming so specific that Treasury Secretary Wolcott complained: "The management of the Treasury becomes more and more difficult. The legislature will not pass laws in gross. Their appropriations are minute; Gallatin, to whom they yield, is evidently intending to break down this department, by charging it with an impracticable detail."[5]

Even Gallatin recognized the need for some executive discretion: "It is impossible for the Legislature to foresee, in all its details, the necessary application of moneys; and a reasonable discretion should be allowed to the proper executive department."[6] This attitude was reinforced when Jefferson appointed Gallatin to be his secretary of the treasury in 1801. A tendency inherent in the executive is the pursuit of more discretion so that it can use its own best judgment to carry out the laws. In the budgetary context a major technique for this purpose is the transfer of funds between appropriation items. This practice had been firmly established by 1801 and continued to grow, even with Gallatin as secretary of treasury.[7]

This was the most common technique used when the executive branch wanted to spend funds for purposes other than those specified in appropriations acts. The other main technique of increasing executive control was that of requesting deficiency funds, presenting Congress with a fait accompli by having already spent those provided and needing additional funds to continue to operate. Representative Hemenway complained that the departments "can make these deficiencies, and Congress can refuse to allow them; but after they are made it is very hard to refuse to allow them."[8]

A major theme of the struggle of the president and Congress over budgetary power is the differing perspective of the two branches. Such a conflict is built into the separation of powers system. Congress, being the policy maker, sees the threat of inroads on its prerogatives when funds are used in ways not foreseen in legislation. Yet the executive naturally feels that it knows more about how it should use funds to best accomplish the purposes for which they were appropriated. Therefore, in dealing with a system of detailed and seemingly restrictive appropriations the executive "continually strove to break the fetters of an unworkable system."[9] Despite these tactics of the executive branch, Congress played the dominant role in federal spending in the nineteenth century.

The Move To Reform and the Executive Budget

The deteriorating condition that existed in federal budgeting in the latter part of the nineteenth century was due to three main factors: (1) the splintering of fiscal power in the Congress, (2) administrative attempts to circumvent congressional control, and (3) "chronic" surpluses created by tariff revenues. Since the Civil War, the appropriations function in

Congress had been split from the revenue raising function. Thus no one unit had authority to examine expenditures and receipts and to try to bring the two into balance. In addition, the dispersal of the power of the Appropriations Committee to other committees resulted in even fewer constraints on spending. As a result congressional spending became more undisciplined, particularly in appropriations for rivers and harbors projects, traditionally a great source of pork barrel.[10] In 1889 James Bryce was moved to say:

> More money is wasted in this way than what the parsimony of the appropriations committee can save. Each of the other standing committees, including the committee on pensions, a source of infinite waste, proposes grants of money, not knowing or heeding what is being proposed by other committees and guided by the executive no further than the members choose.[11]

The pension system created another heavy drain on the treasury.[12] Laws were poorly written and many private bills were introduced, in addition to widespread fraud on the part of claimants.[13]

Although the spate of spending by Congress was under attack by a series of vetos from the president, the executive branch was guilty of its own raids on the treasury. The practice of transferring funds, which had been established in the early years of the republic, was continued, limiting Congress' ability to oversee expenditures.[14] The tactic of coercive deficiencies was also used extensively. Agencies would spend their funds for the year and threaten Congress with the cessation of essential services if additional funds were not provided.[15]

Ironic to any observer of twentieth century fiscal policy is the third factor that contributed to the budgetary chaos of the late nineteenth century: "chronic" budget surpluses. The protective customs tariff was the main source of government revenue, and the large volume of trade insured abundant funds for governmental expenditure. Even with the great strain placed upon the budget by the Civil War, the rapidly expanding economy absorbed the disruption easily. Since there was no internal tax to act as a political counterweight, there was not much effective pressure on the Congress or the executive branch for economy and efficiency. Thus Congress could afford to be lax in its spending measures, and executive agencies could continue to demand deficiency appropriations with impunity. "It is straining human nature too far to expect economy in the face of a budget surplus."[16] James Bryce observed, "Under the system of Congressional finance here described America wastes millions annually. But her wealth is so great, her revenue so elastic that she is not sensible of the loss. She has the glorious privilege of youth, the privilege of committing errors without suffering from their consequences."[17] But the habits formed during the years of surplus continued after the surpluses disappeared and contributed to the demands for an executive budget and more discipline in federal spending.

In 1910 Congress passed a law establishing the Taft Commission on Economy and Efficiency, which would study the national budget system and how it might be reformed.[18] In 1912 the Taft Commission came out with its report, in which it criticized existing practices and went on to recommend a comprehensive executive budget system.[19] The report argued that the executive system would provide for a coherent consideration of revenues and expenditures by the president. After the president formulated his budget plan, he would submit it to the Congress for its action. Budget items would be classified into functional categories; this would make choices among policy priorities more apparent. The report also recommended that Congress deal only with policy direction, leaving implementation to executive expertise.[20] The commission concluded that its proposals constituted "a plan whereby the President and the Congress may cooperate—the one in laying before Congress and the country a clearly expressed administrative program to be acted on, the other in laying before the President a definite enactment to be acted on by him."[21]

Despite widespread support for a national budget system, the Taft Commission recommendations were not enacted into law during his administration. In 1916 the platforms of the three major parties recommended reform of the national budget system.[22] The final impetus for reform came from the economic pressure of World War I, during which expenditures rose from $700 million to $18.5 billion.[23] Support for the executive budget, however, was not unanimous. In 1918 Edward A. Fitzpatrick warned, "The so-called 'executive budget' program proposes a shifting of the center of gravity of our government. Its tendency is toward autocratic executive power. It would achieve this change in government as a by-product to the budget scheme."[24] The developments he predicted were only to occur much later, when President Nixon had maximized the powers merely implicit in the concept of the executive budget. Fitzpatrick wanted to make government more accountable to the people, yet other reformers saw the strengthening of the presidency as a way this could be done. If responsibility were fixed, blame or credit for outcomes could be focused. But the major source of support for the national budget system came from conservatives who were interested in economy and efficiency, which in turn might lead to tax cuts.[25]

In 1919, the House of Representatives created a Select Committee on the Budget under the chairmanship of James W. Good. The committee held extensive hearings and that same year reported out a bill that would reform the national budget system and establish an executive budget. In the report was an assessment of the existing system, specifying the defects the Good bill would remedy.

> Expenditures are not considered in connection with revenues; . . . Congress does not require of the President any carefully thought out financial and work program representing what provision in his opinion should be made for meeting the financial needs of the Government; . . . the estimates of expenditure needs now submitted to Congress represent only the desires of the individual departments, establishments, and bureaus . . . without any superior revision with a view to bringing them into harmony with each other . . . or of making them, as a whole, conform to the needs of the Nation as represented by the Treasury and prospective revenues.[26]

The bill passed the House, 285 to 3, reflecting the support it had from differing political perspectives, including fiscal conservatives and progressive reformers. When it went to the Senate it was modified so that the secretary of the treasury rather than the president would be responsible for preparing the budget. In conference the compromise finally agreed upon made the president responsible for preparing the budget, but the newly established Bureau of the Budget was placed in the Department of the Treasury.

The 1921 Budget and Accounting Act gave the president the authority to transmit a national budget to the Congress each year with supplemental or deficiency estimates, if necessary. The Bureau of the Budget (BOB) was empowered "to assemble, correlate, revise, reduce, or increase the estimates of the several departments or establishments."[27] Thus the president could deny agency requests if they were not consonant with his policy priorities, and agencies were explicitly forbidden to submit spending proposals to Congress, except at its request. In addition to its budgetary functions, BOB was given the mandate to assess management practices in executive agencies and recommend changes in the interest of economy and efficiency. It was understood that Congress would change its procedures to complement the new act; in 1920 the House consolidated jurisdiction for all spending in the Appropriations Committee, and in 1922 the Senate did the same.

The reforms that had been brewing for several decades had finally been institutionalized in 1921. The overall change to correct the ills of the past resulted in a significant increase in the president's power in the budgetary process. Congress had not acted with restraint. It was hoped the president would impose discipline and he was given the tools to do so. In the decades since 1921 the president has come not only to direct but to dominate the federal budgetary process.

The Executive Budget and Central Control

The Budget and Accounting Act of 1921 marked the beginning of the domination of the budgetary process by the institutionalized presidency. It was clear from the act that Congress intended the president to centralize and coordinate requests for funds from the government and submit them to Congress as a package. What was not clear was how this authority would be used and to what extent these new functions would allow the president to expand his institutionalized power. The act called for the president through the Bureau of the Budget to coordinate fiscal policy, but it was also to make studies for the purpose of "securing greater economy and efficiency in the conduct of the public service."[28] These reports could recommend changes in organization, appropriations, or functions of agencies. In the future the expansion of the management function of the bureau was to be based in part on this section.[29]

The growth of presidential dominance in national policy making has been integrally related to the development of the institution of legislative clearance, that is, the necessity to clear legislative proposals from the executive branch with the Budget Bureau before they can be sent to Congress. This section considers the informal practices and formal reorganizations that played roles in the accretion of power to the presidency that took place since the 1921 act.

After signing the new act in June 1921, President Harding appointed Charles G. Dawes to be the first director of the Budget Bureau. Dawes began to organize the bureau and in December issued Budget Circular 49, which initiated the process of central clearance. The circular stated that all agency proposals for legislation, "the effect of which would be to create a charge upon the public treasury or commit the government to obligations which would later require appropriations," must be submitted to the Budget Bureau before congressional action was sought.[30] New proposals could only be put forward with the approval of BOB, and agency opinions on pending legislation would have to include a position statement of the bureau. Executive agencies reacted negatively and Harding backpedalled, assuring them that only routine affairs would be handled without direct presidential action.

Harding did not use the central clearance power very actively, but when Coolidge took office it became an important tool of presidential power. A major goal of President Coolidge was the pursuit of economy and reduction of public expenditures. He used central clearance quite actively to achieve this purpose, though it was confined to legislative proposals costing money and did not reach substantive matters. Any proposals recommending new expenditures would receive careful scrutiny and very likely would be found "in conflict" with the president's program.[31] The same style of clearance policy was practiced through President Hoover's term. The system was not used to coordinate substantive policy, but merely to minimize expenditures.[32]

With the coming of the Great Depression President Roosevelt took a more active role in the budget at the same time that the national government was taking a more active role in the economy.[33] In 1933, acting pursuant to the Economy Act of that year,[34] President Roosevelt issued Executive Order 6166.[35] The purpose of the order was to modify the Antideficiency Act of 1905, which gave department heads the authority to apportion funds throughout the fiscal year in order to prevent premature expenditure of funds and resulting deficiencies. The 1933 order transferred the functions of "making, waiving, and modifying apportionments of appropriations" from department heads to the budget director.[36]

In 1934 President Roosevelt took an important step in the development of central legislative clearance. At a National Emergency Council meeting he announced that he wanted all proposals for legislation to be cleared before going to Congress, not just those concerning expenditures. "Coming down to legislation there has never been any clearing house . . . and, I think in the last analysis that has got to be tried in and go through the National Emergency Council . . . and up to me if necessary. In all probability it will come down to me."[37] This proposal was solidified in 1935 in Budget Circular 336, which provided that legislation "solely concerning policy matters" be referred to the president through the staff of the National Emergency Council.[38] Roosevelt used the new procedures primarily in a negative manner, categorizing proposed legislation as unacceptable, acceptable, or "must" legislation, with only the latter category receiving presidential support. The process was, however, a major innovation in the growing powers of the presidency.

With the slowing down of the New Deal came the decline in importance of the National Emergency Council and its role in legislative clearance. In 1937, Budget Circular 336 was superseded by Circular 344, which provided that substantive legislative proposals even without fiscal implications would be routed to the Budget Bureau for clearance.[39] In 1938 Budget Director Bell allocated a full time staff to coordinate legislation. In addition, that year the Budget Bureau came to control all agency recommendations concerning the signature or veto of enrolled bills. This procedure was formalized in 1939 by Circular 346.[40]

President Roosevelt had appointed a study group consisting of Louis Brownlow, Charles E. Merriam, and Luther Gulick to examine the management of the federal government and to make recommendations for its improvement. The president's Committee on Administrative Management submitted its report to President Roosevelt on January 8, 1937, and on January 12 he passed the suggestions on in a special message to Congress. The committee recommended a five-point program, which included an expansion of the White House staff, the development of the managerial agencies of government, an extension of the merit system, the institution of independent agencies into one of several major executive departments, and the establishment of independent postaudits of all fiscal transactions by an auditor general.[41]

The proposal was in the tradition of twentieth century reform recommendations for the national government: to increase the responsibility and authority of the executive branch. This could appeal to liberals who favored increased accountability and further social legislation, and to conservatives who favored tighter fiscal control for increased economy and efficiency. In the words of the committee, "Stated in simple terms these canons of efficiency require the establishment of a responsible and effective chief executive as the center of energy, direction, and administrative management."[42] In recommending the changes to Congress Roosevelt argued that the reforms conformed with the constitutional separation of powers. "What I am placing before you is not a request for more power, but for the tools of management and for the authority to distribute the work so that the President can effectively discharge those powers which the Constitution now places upon him."[43]

The proposals of the Brownlow committee were debated in Congress and were taken into account in the Reorganization Act of 1939. The act provided that the president could propose plans to Congress to transfer functions from one agency to another, to consolidate functions, or to abolish agencies. The proposed reorganization was to go into effect automatically if it was not disapproved by a majority of both houses of Congress within ten days.[44] The first plan under the act created the Executive Office of the Presidency and placed the Budget Bureau within it, transferring it from the Department of the Treasury.

In 1935 the Budget Bureau still had less than forty employees,[45] but with its expanded duties under the reorganization and the pressure from World War II, the number increased sharply to about six hundred.[46] The reorganization brought new functions and duties to BOB, emphasizing the coordination of all governmental activities in terms of the president's program.[47] These included clearance of recommendations to the president concerning executive orders and proclamations, as well as proposed legislation and an increased attention to administrative problems throughout the federal government.

In 1940 there was also a significant step in the direction of more centralized fiscal control with the issuance of Executive Order 8512 of August 1940. According to the order, federal agencies were to submit to the Treasury Department accounting data, the form and contents of which were to be determined by BOB. This provided for uniform accounting and central reporting for the federal government. In addition, agencies were to submit monthly reports on the status of each appropriation, allowing the bureau to monitor the current status of expenditures and obligations throughout the federal bureaucracy.[48]

Toward the end of World War II, however, the function of coordinating federal activities gravitated toward the Office of War Mobilization (OWM). When Truman came to office he had not had the relationship with BOB that Roosevelt had had, and he came to depend on the OWM. By the end of the war its role had expanded to include more than merely high policy decisions; and Truman turned to it for advice on postwar legislative problems, leaving the Budget Bureau little voice in policy making. In 1946, however, the Office of War Mobilization and Reconversion, as it was renamed,[49] was terminated, leaving the Budget Bureau as the only body able to perform the central coordinating functions for the president. Budget Director Webb played an important role in coordination with the White House, paving the way for BOB's reassertion of its central clearance role.[50]

The Presidency and Central Clearance

In the 1950s BOB continued to play its role of close control over executive branch legislative proposals to the Congress.[51] In the 1960s, however, the role of the Budget Bureau as the policy tool of the president was to decline.[52] Presidents Kennedy and Johnson placed a high value on actively pushing their legislative programs and the career bureaucrats at BOB did not suit their needs.[53] Consequently they relied heavily on their personal White House staff with Theodore Sorenson coordinating for Kennedy and Joseph Califano for Johnson. The role of legislative clearance on important matters was taken from the Budget Bureau into the White House.[54] In the 1960s the role of primary policy tool in fiscal matters for the president was performed by the White House staff rather than by BOB. "The Bureau's failure to orient itself to the service of the President was due largely to its institutional status. As it became the institutionalized Presidency, the Bureau became separated from the President."[55]

In April 1969, shortly after coming to office, President Nixon created the President's Advisory Council on Executive Organization and appointed Roy Ash its chairman. It was to examine the organization of the executive branch and recommend changes that would make it more effective in carrying out policy. After receiving Ash's report and also considering the 1967 report of a BOB steering group,[56] Nixon submitted Reorganization Plan 2 of 1970 to Congress. Neither house disapproved the plan and it went into effect on July 1, 1970. It created the Domestic Council "to coordinate policy formulation in the domestic area" and the Office of Management and Budget (OMB). "The Domestic Council will be primarily concerned with *what* we do; the Office of Management and Budget will be primarily concerned with *how* we do it, and *how well* we do it."[57] OMB would have a budget section and a management section, and would replace the old BOB.

The main purpose of the reorganization was to institutionalize in the Domestic Council the White House staff role in legislative clearance and to make the Budget Bureau more amenable to presidential direction. One of the aspects of BOB Nixon wanted to change was the close relationship between career budget officers and the agencies with whom they worked. He also wanted to put much more control of the budget into the hands of political appointees rather than career civil servants who might not be as committed to the president's program.[58] To accomplish this the program divisions were put under the supervision of associate directors who were political appointees rather than career civil servants. Accordingly, direct policy input would come at a lower level in OMB than had been the case in the Bureau of the Budget.

One of the major changes that resulted from the 1970 reorganization was that the function of central legislative clearance passed from the legislative reference section to the associate directors. Phillip Hughes, chief of legislative reference from 1958 to 1966, and Roger W. Jones, chief from 1949 to 1957, made policy decisions themselves. Wilfred H. Rommel (carried over from the Johnson administration as chief of legislative reference under Nixon) did technical work on legislation, but had little input in policy formulation. Most policy decisions were made by the political appointees or, in particularly important issues, by the Domestic Council.[59] In addition, a change was instituted in the nature of decisions on budget requests from agencies. Under the old system the decision on budget allocations for agencies was made by the budget director but could be appealed over his head to the president. Under President Nixon's budget director, George Schultz, the figure given to the agencies was presented as the president's decision. This made appeal much more difficult and unlikely. It would be tantamount to asking the president to review his own decision.

Although BOB had always been the tool of the president in office and advocate for his policies, the career bureaucrats were considered to have a high degree of professionalism and technical competence. After Nixon's reorganization, however, political appointees in the new middle level of the hierarchy were placed at crucial points of leverage and communication. These people were sometimes recruited from outside the government and some had little sensitivity to the constitutional position of Congress in the budgetary process.[60]

The result was an OMB that was perceived to be more politicized than BOB had been under other presidents and more responsive to Richard Nixon than to the institution of the presidency. Hugh Heclo has concluded that "developments in the Nixon years left much less separation between the OMB's budget judgements and the President's personal position."[61] A panel of the National Academy of Public Administration stated that a "powerful White House staff which has progressively assumed the role of speaking for the President has seriously diminished the responsibilities of the career, professional staff of OMB and its capacity to provide the kind of objective and expert counsel to the President which characterized earlier operations."[62]

Notes

1. *The Federalist Papers* (New York: The New American Library, 1961), no. 58, p. 359.

2. Edward S. Corwin, *The President* (New York: New York University Press, 1957), p. 128.

3. Joseph P. Harris, *Congressional Control of Administration* (Washington, D.C.: Brookings Institution, 1964), p. 49.

4. Quoted in Murray L. Weidenbaum and John S. Saloma, *Congress and the Federal Budget* (Washington, D.C.: American Enterprise Institute, 1965), p. 110. See also Lucius Wilmerding, Jr., *The Spending Power* (New Haven, Conn.: Yale University Press, 1943), Chap. 2.

5. Quoted in Wilmerding, *The Spending Power*, p. 46.

6. Ibid., p. 38.

7. Weidenbaum and Saloma, *Congress,* pp. 110-11.

8. U.S., Congress, *Congressional Record,* 39, p. 3687.

9. Arthur Smithies, *The Budgetary Process in the United States* (New York: McGraw-Hill, 1955), p. 54.

10. See Louis Fisher, *President and Congress* (New York: The Free Press, 1972), pp. 92-97.

11. *The American Commonwealth* (1922 ed.), 1:180, quoted in Harris, *Congressional Control,* p. 55.

12. See Fisher, *President and Congress,* pp. 95-96.

13. This has led Fisher to characterize the presidency during this period as the "Protector of the Purse"; see ibid., p. 95.

14. For congressional reaction to transfers of funds and other administrative tactics, see Wilmerding, *The Spending Power,* Chapter 6, "The Anger of Congress," pp. 118-36.

15. See ibid., Chapter 7, "The Fight Against Deficiencies," pp.137-53.

16. Smithies, *The Budgetary Process,* p. 59.

17. *The American Commonwealth,* 1:184, quoted in Harris, *Congressional Control,* p. 55.

18. See Percival Flack Brundage, *The Bureau of the Budget* (New York: Praeger, 1970), p. 7.

19. U.S., Congress, House, Taft Commission on Economy and Efficiency, *The Need for a National Budget System,* 62d Cong., 2d sess., 1912, H. Doc. 854.

20. See Smithies, *The Budgetary Process,* pp. 68-71.

21. Quoted in Harris, *Congressional Control,* p. 58.

22. Fisher, *President and Congress,* p. 101.

23. Ibid.

24. *Budget Making in a Democracy* (New York: Macmillan Company, 1918), quoted in Jesse Burkhead, *Government Budgeting* (New York: John Wiley and Sons, Inc., 1956), p. 25.

25. See Burkhead, *Government Budgeting,* p. 26.

26. U.S., Congress, House, Select Committee on the Budget, *National Budget System,* 66th Cong., 1st sess., 1919, H. Rept. 362 to Accompany H. Rept. 9783, p. 4, quoted in Harris, *Congressional Control,* p. 60.

27. Quoted in Fritz Morstein Marx, "The Bureau of the Budget: Its Evolution and Present Role," Part I, *American Political Science Review* 39, no. 4 (1954):668.

28. 44 Stat. 20, Sec. 209. See also Marx, "The Bureau of the Budget," Part 2, p. 887.

29. See Marx, "The Bureau of the Budget," Part 1, pp. 668-72, and passim.

30. Quoted in Richard E. Neustadt, "Presidency and Legislation: The Growth of Central Clearance," *American Political Science Review* 48, no. 3 (1954):644.

31. Ibid., p. 646.

32. Ibid., p. 647.

33. See Brundage, *The Bureau of the Budget,* pp. 19-23.

34. 48 Stat. 8.

35. U.S., Congress, *Congressional Record,* 10 June 1933, 77, p. 5708.

36. Mary Louise Ramsey, "Impoundment by the Executive Department of Funds which Congress Has Authorized it to Spend or Obligate," U.S., Library of Congress, Legislative Reference Service (1968), in U.S., Congress, Senate, Committee on the Judiciary, Subcommittee on Separation of Powers, *Executive Impoundment of Appropriated Funds,* Hearings, 92d Cong., 1st sess., March 1971, p. 569.

37. National Emergency Council, "Proceedings of the Nineteenth Meeting" (Washington, D.C.: National Emergency Council, 11 December 1934), "Central Clearance," p. 649.

38. Ibid., pp. 649-50.

39. See Marx, "The Bureau of the Budget," Part 2, p. 881; and Neustadt, "Central Clearance," p. 653.

40. Neustadt, "Central Clearance," pp. 654-57.

41. See Rexford G. Tugwell, *The Enlargement of the Presidency* (New York: Doubleday, 1960), pp. 303-4.

42. Quoted in Smithies, *The Budgetary Process,* p. 79.

43. Quoted in Tugwell, *Enlargement,* p. 404.

44. See Brundage, *The Bureau of the Budget,* p. 25.

45. Marx, "The Bureau of the Budget," Part 1, p. 683.

46. Brundage, *The Bureau of the Budget,* p. 29.

47. Marx, "The Bureau of the Budget," Part 1, p. 683.

48. See Marx, "The Bureau of the Budget," Part 2, p. 877.

49. By the War Mobilization and Recovery Act of 1944.

50. See Neustadt, "Central Clearance," pp. 657-60.

51. See Joel Havemann, "OMB's legislative role is growing more powerful and more political," *National Journal Reports* (27 October 1973):1595, 1599; Robert S. Gilmour, "Central Legislative Clearance: A Revised Perspective," *Public Administrative Review* 31 (March/April 1971):152, and Neustadt, "Central Clearance," pp. 664-68.

52. See Allen Schick, "The Budget Bureau that Was: Thoughts on the Rise, Decline, and Future of a Presidential Agency," *Law and Contemporary Problems* (1974):519.

53. See Gilmour, "Revised Perspective," p. 156; and Havemann, "OMB's role," p. 1595.

54. See Gilmour, "Revised Perspective," p. 152; and Schick, "The Budget Bureau that Was," pp. 532-33.

55. Schick, "The Budget Bureau that Was," p. 532.

56. Ibid., p. 534.

57. Reorganization Plan 2 of 1970, in Robert T. Golembiewski et al., *Public Administration* (Chicago: Rand McNally, 1972), p. 410.

58. See Dom Bonafede, "The making of the President's budget; politics and influence in a new manner," *National Journal Reports* 3 (23 January 1971):151; and Havemann, "OMB's role," p. 1595.

59. Havemann, "OMB's role," pp. 1590, 1595-6. See John H. Kessel, *The Domestic Presidency: Decision-making in the White House* (N. Scituate, Massachusetts: Duxbury, 1975).

60. Louis Fisher, *Presidential Spending Power* (Princeton, N.J.: Princeton University Press, 1975), p. 56.

61. Hugh Heclo, "OMB and the Presidency—the problem of 'neutral competence'," *The Public Interest,* no. 38 (Winter 1975):87.

62. Quoted in Fisher, *Presidential Spending Power,* p. 56.

3

Impoundment as a Presidential Policy Tool

Introduction

As the embodiment of the separation of powers system, the Constitution provides that the spending power shall be shared by Congress and the president, although the Congress is considered to have the purse.[1] In money matters generally, the Constitution provides: "The Congress shall have the Power To lay and collect Taxes, Duties, Imposts and Excises, to pay the Debts and provide for the common defense and general Welfare of the United States."[2] In addition to the power to raise revenue, all other powers relating to money are also vested in Congress. They include the power to borrow money, to regulate commerce, to legislate concerning bankruptcy, to coin money, and to regulate its value.

It is the duty of the executive, however, to actually spend the money. The provision that "no money shall be drawn from the Treasury, but in consequence of appropriations made by law"[3] assumes that expenditure is primarily a function of the executive.[4] Its main purpose seems to have been to ensure that the president was accountable to Congress by not giving him an independent source of revenue. However, the question has arisen: is the president *obligated* to spend money pursuant to legislative appropriations?

This chapter describes the budgetary process and various mechanisms that have been set up in legislation to spend funds. Presidential refusal to expend funds can occur at several stages of the process and for a variety of reasons. These issues will be examined and different types of impoundment actions will be distinguished. The remainder of the chapter examines the use of the impoundment by various presidents throughout U.S. history. Most presidents did not impound funds in amounts significant to be noticeable, although every president since Franklin Roosevelt has refused to spend funds in important ways. But President Nixon impounded funds in ways significantly different from all other presidents.

This historical analysis is important for several reasons. The use of impoundment as a presidential tool did not spring up full-blown at one time; it was developed over a period of several decades. In order to understand recent usage and its departure from previous practices, it is necessary to understand how the technique was used in the past. In addition, President Nixon justified his impoundments by claiming that other presidents engaged in similar practices. It is important to examine past impoundments in order to intelligently weigh arguments based on historical precedent.

The Definition and Use of Impoundment

Impoundment of funds has been characterized by Deputy Attorney General Sneed as "not spending money,"[5] and in its broadest sense, impoundment is the refusal by the executive to spend funds provided by Congress. The proposed Senate antiimpoundment bill, S. 373, defined impoundment broadly and included "any type of Executive action or inaction which effectively precludes or delays the obligation or expenditure of any part of authorized budget authority."[6] The purpose of impoundment can be accomplished in several different ways and at several different points in the budgetary process.

The process by which the federal government spends money involves the president and Congress in a complex series of decisions. The president may propose the expenditure of funds, which he does primarily through his annual budget message. After Congress has acted, the executive branch must then do the actual spending. But the congressional budget process makes the basic spending decisions for the government.

In general there are two steps in the congressional process:

authorization and appropriation.[7] Authorizations are reported by legislative committees, which recommend the level of budget authority for programs within their jurisdiction. Budget authority, which allows federal agencies to enter into obligations, is usually not provided by authorizations, but by appropriations, which are reported by the appropriations committees. No money may be appropriated unless it is first authorized, though oftentimes the funds finally appropriated are considerably less than those authorized. Authorizations may be provided annually, in multiple years, or for an indefinite period. If the funds are not spent during the time for which they were appropriated, they revert to the general treasury.

An appropriations act permits a federal government unit to incur obligations and directs the treasury to pay them. The appropriations committees decide how much money may be spent by providing budget authority, which is defined as "authority provided by law to enter into obligations which will result in immediate or future outlays involving Government funds."[8] Ordinarily budget authority can only be created by legislation originating from the appropriations committees. But through the procedure of backdoor spending, some legislative committees can report legislation providing budget authority. This is done in three main ways: contract authority, borrowing authority, and mandatory entitlements.

Contract authority allows agencies to enter into contracts before funds are actually appropriated. These are legal obligations and money must be appropriated when the payments fall due. Borrowing authority allows federal agencies to spend money by incurring debts. Mandatory entitlements are laws that give certain persons legal rights to funds if they fall within certain categories. Major entitlement programs include veterans' benefits, social security payments, and the food stamp program. Congress cannot foresee how many claims will be made and must appropriate enough money to cover all legal claims.

After the Congress has provided for the expenditure of funds by creating budget authority, it is up to the executive branch to actually spend them. It is at this point that the impoundment technique can be applied. The president has in some cases merely ordered a department head not to allow the expenditure of certain funds. This happened when Howard Phillips, as acting director of the Office of Economic Opportunity, refused to release funds as part of a plan to dismantle the whole program.[9] There are also other means by which the prevention of certain expenditures can be achieved, depending upon the spending mechanisms that have been set up in legislation.

Some legislation, such as the Federal Aid Highway Act of 1956[10] and the Federal Water Pollution Control Act Amendments of 1972,[11] has set up a two-stage spending process. In this procedure the money is first allotted among the states according to a formula fixed in the law. The states plan how the money is to be utilized and then submit the plans to the appropriate department. If the plans are subsequently approved, the states are allowed to enter into contracts based upon the plans.

One of the techniques that has been used to preclude the expenditure of funds is the refusal to allot the funds initially. Since contracts cannot be let before funds are allotted, the money is effectively impounded. The Supreme Court has ruled that such actions were illegal in the administration of the 1972 Water Pollution Control Act Amendments.[12]

Funds can also be withheld by the refusal of the proper executive officials to approve plans submitted by the states. Of course, some plans may be disapproved because they are inadequate according to departmental regulations. But in certain cases departments have effectively impounded funds by refusing, across the board, to approve plans. Such actions were challenged in court by the State Highway Commission of Missouri. The Eighth Circuit Court of Appeals ruled that it was illegal for the Department of Transportation to reject plans for reasons other than those based on the language of the act. This meant that funds could no longer be withheld because of inflation or the general state of the economy as the Nixon administration had been doing.

Impoundment can also be effected by the refusal of administrative officials to accept and process applications for funds from other governmental units. Several district courts have ruled that such refusals violate the laws that mandate the administration of the programs involved.[13] The definitions and categories of impounding actions established in the 1974 Budget Act will be discussed in Chapter 7.

Presidential Impoundment Practice

Impoundments have been accomplished by all of the above-mentioned techniques and at several different points in the budgetary process, but the practice was not established at any particular time or by any specific statute. Rather, like many practices of U.S. governmental institutions, it developed incrementally over several decades. Although in 1803 President Jefferson deferred for one year monies provided for purchasing gunboats[14] and President Grant refused to spend some rivers and harbors funds,[15] impoundment has been largely a twentieth-century practice. Its use has developed since the establishment of the executive budget in 1921 and has paralleled the growth of presidential control over the budget.

Its development can be divided into five stages which follow a chronological order and show increasing control asserted by the president over spending.[16]

- Stage 1, the use of apportionment to effect savings;
- Stage 2, the control of the level of program implementation;
- Stage 3, cancellation of particular projects;
- Stage 4, military impoundments; and
- Stage 5, prospective impoundment and the cancellation of whole programs (innovations of President Nixon).

The Nixon impoundments also differed from those of all previous presidents in other significant ways, which will be specified.

Stage 1: Apportionment to Effect Savings

The Bureau of the Budget was established in 1921; President Harding's first budget director was Charles W. Dawes. The Antideficiency Act of 1905 had required department heads to apportion funds throughout the year so as to prevent deficiencies. Dawes interpreted the act to allow reserves to be made for purposes of savings. Immediately after the establishment of the Budget Bureau Dawes issued Budget Circular 4, which ordered each department head to list expenditures that were indispensable during the year. The remainder of the appropriations were to go into a "general reserve." Further savings were to be made, if possible, and placed in the reserve.[17] Although Dawes did not consider appropriations to mandate expenditures of the full amount of funds, he did not believe that department heads or the president could control the level of expenditures at their will. His primary aims were administrative efficiency and economy while still accomplishing the will of Congress.

> The Budget Bureau has no control of policy and is concerned simply with economy and efficiency in the routine business of government. The Bureau of the Budget is simply a business organization whose activities are devoted constantly to the consideration of how money appropriated by Congress can be made to go as far as possible toward the accomplishment of the objects of legislation.[18]

Stage 2: Controlling the Rate of Program Implementation

The second stage began in the early 1930s. In an attempt to alleviate the pressure from the depression, President Hoover ordered a 10 percent cut in overall expenditures. He used the procedures set up under Dawes in which each department was asked to cut its proposed expenditures by 10 percent, the savings making up a reserve that could only be used with presidential approval.

During this second stage Hoover used his power to effect savings to control the tempo or rate of program implementation. In addition, he received statutory authority to reorganize federal agencies, reduce salaries of officials, and make partial layoffs in order to effect a savings that would revert to the general treasury.[19] By the mid-1930s the Budget Bureau was controlling the rate of implementation not only of overall expenditures but also of specific programs. Presidential control was further strengthened in 1933 when Executive Order

6166 transferred the authority to apportion appropriations from department heads to the Budget Bureau.

Stage 3: Cancellation of Particular Projects

The third stage of development was initiated by Franklin Roosevelt and marked the emergence of impoundment as a politically controversial issue. In 1939, the Budget Bureau was shifted to the Executive Office of the President, giving the president tighter control over executive bureaucracies.[20] President Roosevelt put this control to use when the economy began to shift to war production and the price index began to rise. There was a problem with inflation, and resources had to be shifted to war production. In order to accomplish these purposes Franklin D. Roosevelt stated in his budget message of January 3, 1941: "During this period of national emergency, it seems appropriate to defer *construction projects* that interfere with the defense program by diverting manpower and materials" (emphasis added).[21]

There were limited impoundments in the late 1930s, primarily reducing the level of programs.[22] In the early 1940s BOB impounded funds from projects low in defense priorities. They included appropriations for the Civilian Conservation Corps, surplus labor force, civilian-pilot training projects, the Surplus Marketing Corporation, and other projects not related to defense.[23] In 1941 Congress ignored President Roosevelt's budgetary wishes and attached some flood control projects—not considered by the administration to be essential to the national defense—to the War Department Civil Appropriation Act for 1942.[24] Having no item veto, Franklin D. Roosevelt signed the bill but warned that he did not intend to spend funds not essential for defense. In spite of the president's wish, additional funds were provided by the Congress for nonapproved flood control projects, including a flood control levee on the Arkansas River at Tulsa, Oklahoma, and a power and control reservoir at Markham Ferry, Oklahoma. Under the president's direction, Budget Director Harold Smith announced that funds for the two projects would be impounded, unless the Office of Production Management presented evidence that the projects were essential to national defense.[25]

In justifying the impoundment of funds, President Roosevelt said in a letter to Richard Russell, a member of the Senate Appropriations Committee:

> While our statutory system of fund apportionment is not a substitute for an item or blanket veto power, and should not be used to set aside or nullify the expressed will of Congress, I cannot believe that you or Congress as a whole would take exception to either of these purposes which are common to sound business management everywhere.[26]

The letter was meant to allay growing congressional criticism of the Budget Bureau's impoundment of funds. In October 1942, however, a steel mill near Tulsa became damaged in a flood and the War Production Board (WPB) certified that the levee was essential to national defense. The funds were released by the Budget Bureau. The Bureau, however, continued to withhold funds for the Markham Ferry project.[27]

Congressional reaction to President Roosevelt's impoundment policy was gathering momentum. When Congress passed a bill in the summer of 1943 for aiding states constructing rural post roads, Senator McKellar added a rider (Section 9). It provided that "No part of any appropriation authorized in this act shall be impounded or withheld from obligation or expenditure by any agency or official other than the Commission of Public Roads."[28] In conference the amendment was changed to allow impoundment only on certification by WPB that a particular project would hurt the war effort. McKellar had achieved at least a minor limitation on BOB's power to impound.

In the fall of 1943 Budget Director Smith was questioned by senators about BOB impoundment in hearings about a supplemental appropriations bill for defense. Unsatisfied by Smith's defense of impoundment practices. McKellar attached a legislative rider to the National Defense Appropriation Bill (Section 305). It read as follows:

> That no appropriation or part of any appropriation heretofor, herein, or hereafter made available for any executive department or independent establishment to construct any particular

project shall be impounded, or held as a reserve, or used for any
other purpose, except by direction of the Congress, and any part
of such appropriation not needed to complete such project, or
the part thereof for which appropriation has been made, shall be
retained by the Treasury.[29]

The amendment passed the Senate in December 1943 and was
the first general antiimpoundment measure to pass either
house of Congress. The House, being traditionally more
fiscally conservative, and aware that impoundment had
resulted in savings in the early 1940s, rejected the McKellar
amendment.

Stage 4: The Military Impoundments

Military impoundments have been grouped into a separate
category not only because the bulk of them occurred between
the late 1940s and early 1960s, but also because of their special
constitutional nature. The constitutional designation of the
president as commander in chief of the armed forces places his
decisions regarding military spending into a special status that
may give him more legitimacy than he possesses in domestic
spending. The legal and constitutional issues involved in this
distinction will be discussed in the next chapter.

The most salient impoundment by President Truman was
his refusal in 1949 to release funds appropriated for the air
force. The president's request was for a forty-eight–group air
force, but Congress appropriated money for fifty-eight groups.
Despite the congressional appropriation, Truman felt a strong
need to cut expenditures. Secretary of Defense Forrestal was
replaced by Louis Johnson in March 1949, who, along with the
president's domestic advisors, had optimistic expectations
about the prospects of peace. Furthermore, the Eberstadt Task
Force of the Hoover Commission had just concluded that the
Pentagon was being prodigal with its funds. Truman also felt
pressure to cut expenditures following recent tax reductions
that were passed over his veto and a loss of revenue due to the
1948-49 recession.[30]

Truman's response was to sign the appropriations bill but to
direct Secretary of Defense Johnson to withhold the extra $735
million: "you are directed to place in reserve the funds

provided in the National Military Establishment Appropriation Act, 1950, which would permit increasing the structure of the Air Force beyond the program proposed in the 1950 Budget."[31] The extra funds were placed in reserve. The reason Truman gave for his action was that the expenditures would put too much pressure on the peacetime economy. When the Secretary of Defense was questioned in a House appropriations subcommittee hearing about Truman's authority to impound, he said the president's actions were justified by his constitutional powers as chief executive and commander in chief as well as by the Budget and Accounting Act and the "Apportionment Act" (the Antideficiency Act of 1905).[32]

Truman's impoundment was challenged by the House, which cited the constitutional provisions giving Congress war powers and stated that Congress was given the responsibility for the national defense. The report went on to say that the Congress carefully considered the additional ten air force groups it added to the president's request.

> A major question of policy was determined by the Congress, and funds were provided to implement the policy but the will of Congress was circumvented.
> It is all perfectly justifiable and proper for all possible economies to be effected and savings to be made, but there is no warrant or justification for the thwarting of a major policy of Congress by the impounding of funds.[33]

In spite of the House's feelings the funds remained impounded.[34]

Another major impoundment dispute during the Truman presidency was the cancellation of the U.S.S. *United States,* which was to be a super aircraft carrier that could handle long-range bombers. One of the factors involved in its cancellation was the combining of the separate military services into the Department of Defense. Secretary Johnson consulted the Joint Chiefs of Staff and Carl Vinson and Millard Tydings, chairmen of the House and Senate Armed Services Committees, respectively. With their recommendation and President Truman's approval, Johnson cancelled the project. Because of the congressional and Defense Department support, there was no major outcry directed at the impoundment.

Impoundments during President Eisenhower's term in office were concentrated in the area of defense, consistent with his policy of asserting civilian control over the military. His most disputed impoundment action came when the army wanted to develop the $6 billion Nike-Zeus missile system in 1958. Despite technical deficiencies in the system cited by Defense Secretary McElroy, Congress appropriated $135 million in 1959 for initial procurement. Eisenhower impounded the funds and in 1960 said that funds would be used for development, but not for production until the system was free of bugs.[35]

This type of impoundment might be considered a routine, administrative action to ensure that funds are not wasted on projects that were inadequately planned. In fact, in the later years of his administration Eisenhower impounded considerable funds, primarily for routine purposes.[36] These included funds withheld from a number of defense projects, involving appropriations for additional strategic airlift aircraft and the Nike-Zeus procurement.[37] Eisenhower also requested that expenditures be curtailed to stay within the debt limit in fiscal 1958. When the pressure on the debt ceiling was relieved, he released the funds. In fiscal 1959 he requested a two percent reduction in employment level in order to promote efficiency, but this involved no cancellation of any project or function.[38]

The major impoundment controversy during John Kennedy's presidency was over the development of the RS-70 bomber (a modification of the B-70 bomber). Although mandatory language was finally deleted from the bill, the incident is important for the congressional debate that surrounded it. In 1961 the Kennedy administration, in emphasizing a "flexible response" defense posture and in relying upon the U.S. missile deterrent, decided to restrict the B-70 bomber program to the prototype stage.[39] Congress disagreed with Kennedy about strategic priorities in the defense budget and added additional funds to those already requested by the administration. Defense Secretary McNamara refused to release the funds.

The House Armed Services Committee, especially Chairman

Carl Vinson, saw this as a challenge to its role in defense policy making and in March 1962 voted to mandate spending on the project. The Secretary of Defense was "directed, ordered, mandated, and required to utilize the full amount of the $491 million authority granted . . . for an RS-70 weapons systems."[40]

The committee was willing to test wills with the executive: "If this language constitutes a test as to whether Congress has the power to so mandate, let the test be made."[41] The report went on to cite recent defense impoundments and discussed Congress' relationship to the executive.

> The committee finds it hard to believe that its extended and infinitely detailed hearings are designed only as an exercise in self-improvement in the area of *knowledge*. For knowledge is something to be used, not merely to be possessed.
>
> To any student of government, it is eminently clear that the role of the Congress in determining national policy, defense or otherwise, has deteriorated over the years.
>
> Perhaps this is the time, and the RS-70 the occasion, to reverse this trend. Perhaps this is the time to reexamine the role and function of Congress and discover whether it is playing the part that the Founding Fathers ordained that it should.[42]

The House committee saw the issue as an opportunity to begin to right the balance between the president and Congress. However not all members of Congress felt the same way as Vinson did, and Kennedy had lined up congressional leaders, including House Speaker McCormack and Majority Leader Carl Albert to fight the mandatory language on the floor.[43]

President Kennedy, however, did not wish to provoke a clash between Congress and the presidency, and was advised that a floor fight with Vinson would be lost. He thus invited Vinson to the White House for a chat and convinced him to withdraw the mandatory language.[44] In a letter to Vinson he said, "I would respectfully suggest that, in place of the word 'directed,' the word 'authorized' would be more suitable to an authorizing bill (which is not an appropriation of funds) and more clearly in line with the spirit of the Constitution." As a means of conciliation he promised that Secretary McNamara would undertake a study "to reexamine the RS-70 program and related technological possibilities."[45]

Politically, it was clearly a victory for the White House. The constitutional issue was avoided and only two prototypes of the RS-70 were built. One crashed in June 1966 and the other is in the Air Force Museum at Dayton, Ohio.[46] Kennedy's letter emphasized his "responsibilities as President and Commander-in-Chief" and implied that he might have the authority not to spend despite the mandatory language. It has been suggested, however, that the very fact that his administration made such an effort to have the mandatory language deleted implies the recognition that Congress has the power to mandate spending.[47]

President Johnson impounded defense funds and also began impounding domestic funds for non-defense-related reasons.[48] One of the major controversies during the Johnson administration concerned national defense and was similar to the RS-70 incident, except that Congress' will finally prevailed. Again, it was a question of the House Armed Services Committee priorities versus those of the administration. In 1965 a navy request for a nuclear powered guided missile frigate was turned down by the Defense Department and, when Congress authorized $150 million for it anyway, Secretary of Defense McNamara refused to release the funds. In 1967 Chairman L. Mendel Rivers of the House Armed Services Committee decided to use mandatory language for two of the ships in an amendment to the 1967 military procurement authorization bill.[49] "Notwithstanding the provision of any other law, the Secretary of Defense and the Secretary of the Navy shall proceed with the design, engineering, and construction of the two nuclear powered guided missile frigates as soon as practicable."[50] This language passed the whole House by a margin of 356-2. The Senate Armed Services Committee, however, was not committed to forcing the issue and its version did not contain the mandatory language. The bill went to conference and the final wording was closer to the Senate's version: "The contract for the construction of the nuclear powered guided missile frigate . . . shall be entered into as soon as practicable unless the President fully advises the Congress that its construction is not in the national interest."[51]

McNamara then announced that the original $150.5 million would be released for the first ship, though the Department of Defense would not recommend allocation of two more for which the navy and House Armed Services Committee were pushing. Congress disagreed with the secretary and monies were authorized and appropriated for two more frigates in the amount of $155 million.[52] The House Armed Services Committee and Chairman Rivers still saw a threat to congressional prerogatives in the area of defense priorities. "If the reluctance of the Secretary of Defense to accept nuclear propulsion is not overcome shortly, the prime question before the Congress will become: Can the appointed Secretary of Defense thwart the exercise of the constitutional powers of the Congress to provide and maintain a Navy?"[53] McNamara recommended that the funds in question be reprogrammed but the Joint Atomic Energy Committee joined the House Armed Services Committee on the issue of the frigates and finally President Johnson ordered that the two ships be constructed.

Although the issue never actually came to a confrontation, the incident is significant in illustrating the clash of priorities between the president and Congress and the growing feeling in the Congress that its prerogatives were being usurped by the executive branch.

Stage 5: The Nixon Impoundments

The presidential practice of refusing to spend funds provided by Congress had been growing during the twentieth century along with most other powers exercised by the executive branch. President Johnson was the first president to impound large amounts in areas of domestic policy, though this did not provoke clashes with the Democratic Congress. President Nixon's impoundment practices, however, differed from those of all previous presidents in five significant ways, which will be delineated below.

One of the most controversial of President Johnson's impoundments was his withholding of highway trust funds announced in his message to Congress of September 8, 1966. Attorney General Ramsey Clark concluded that, based on the Antideficiency Act and the language of the Federal Aid

Highway Act of 1958, the president was not legally obligated to release the funds.[54] The State of Missouri took the case to court, and the Eighth Circuit Court of Appeals ruled the impoundments to be against the law. A decision handed down on April 12, 1973, stated that "apportioned funds are not to be withheld from obligation for purposes totally unrelated to the highway program."[55]

Many of President Johnson's impoundments were made in an attempt to curb inflation in the mid 1960s. In September 1966 when Congress added $312.5 million more than requested to an agriculture appropriation bill, Johnson signed the bill anyway and announced he would cut expenditures for certain of the items in the bill.[56] In his economic message to Congress in September 1966, he directed that savings be made whenever possible and appropriations in excess of his budget recommendations were to be withheld. After the November elections it became clear that the spending areas affected would be the Highway Trust Fund; HUD; and the department of Health, Education, and Welfare; Agriculture; and the Interior. About half the funds were cancelled and half were released as a result of political pressure from various localities.[57]

The practice of impoundment under President Nixon changed radically from the use of the power by previous presidents. This, along with other factors, contributed to the atmosphere of constitutional crisis surrounding the latter part of President Nixon's administration. Specifically, the Nixon impoundments differed from those of previous presidents in five ways.

First, he impounded larger amounts than other presidents. From 1969 to 1972 the Nixon administration impounded 17 to 20 percent of controllable expenditures, more than any previous administration.[58] Although administration spokesmen claimed their total impoundments constituted a smaller percentage of GNP than the Johnson impoundments, their argument was based on OMB (Office of Management and Budget) figures that excluded large sums (particularly water pollution control funds) that many in Congress considered to be impoundments. If these sums were included, the Nixon impoundments would greatly exceed those of the Johnson

years, which were the largest to that time. Also, while President
Johnson deferred spending funds in domestic areas, many of
the funds were slated for eventual release. By 1973 President
Nixon had impounded funds for over 100 programs, most of
which were to be permanent cuts. Much of the money was
withheld for reasons unrelated to the specific programs, such as
inflation or the general state of the economy.[59]

Second, some Nixon impoundments were made despite
explicit expressions of intent by Congress that the funds be
spent. This was unlike all previous impoundments, with the
exception of those connected with military spending.[60] For
instance, the Federal Aid Highway Act was amended in 1968 to
read in part: "It is the sense of Congress that under existing law
no part of any sums authorized to be appropriated for
expenditure upon any Federal-aid system which has been
apportioned pursuant to the provisions of this title shall be
impounded or withheld from obligation."[61] Yet President
Nixon refused to spend $2.5 of $4.5 billion apportioned in
order to curtail inflation. The override of President Nixon's
veto of the Federal Water Pollution Control Act Amendments
of 1972 indicated that Congress intended to commit significant
national resources to that national problem. Despite the veto
override, 55 percent of the funds for 1973 and 1974 were
withheld.

Third, the Nixon administration used impoundment to try
to terminate entire programs rather than merely particular
projects. This had not been done before in nonmilitary areas.[62]
For instance, in 1972 the Department of Agriculture announced that low interest loans made available by the Rural
Electrification Act of 1936 would be terminated as of January 1,
1973.[63] The loans were used to finance the construction of
electrical equipment for rural areas.[64] The issue was settled by a
compromise in May 1973 with the restoration of part of the
loans.[65] Also in January 1973 Secretary of Agriculture Butz
announced that the Rural Environmental Assistance Program
was being terminated by the impounding of all of its funds.[66] At
the same time the Water Bank Program, which was established
to preserve wetlands for waterfowl, was also terminated.[67]

A fourth departure from precedent of the Nixon administration was the withholding of funds from programs that were not included in its proposed budget. In the fall of 1970 President Nixon signed an authorization bill for sewer and water lines but warned that any appropriations above his recommendations would have a "disastrous fiscal effect." "I must and will act to avoid the harmful fiscal consequences of this legislation. I will be compelled to withhold any overfunding."[68] He carried out his promise and funded the public works projects he had recommended. He deferred, without exception, the additional programs that Congress had added.

In the spring of 1971 OMB announced that it was withholding $12 billion, primarily from highway funds and various urban programs. The reasons for the impounding were that the administration wanted to replace such categorical grant-in-aid programs with bloc grants and general revenue sharing. "This was the administration's way of saying that it intended to implement a program which was not yet law, but would not implement a program already authorized and funded."[69]

On March 4, 1971, Secretary of HUD Romney announced that urban grants-in-aid were being held back because there was no point in spending money on programs that were "scheduled for termination."[70] What he meant was that the administration wanted to consolidate and replace such programs with revenue sharing. Thus the present program was being phased out on the assumption that Congress would enact the administration's budget as requested. The above examples of impounding in a prospective sense had no precedent and were a significant innovation in the shifting of priorities from one administration to the next.[71]

The fifth difference between President Nixon and all previous presidents who impounded funds is that he claimed the formal constitutional power to do so. "The Constitutional right of the President of the United States to impound funds, and that is not to spend money, when the spending of money would mean either increasing prices or increasing taxes for all the people—that right is absolutely clear."[72] President Roosevelt impounded funds but not as a major policy tool. He thought impoundment "should not be used to set aside or nullify the expressed will of Congress."[73] When the Civil Rights Commission proposed that President Kennedy cut off government funds going to institutions practicing racial discrimination, he said, "I don't have the power to cut off the aid in a general way, . . . and I think it would probably be unwise to give the President of the United States that kind of power."[74] Therefore, in addition to the ways in which President Nixon's practice of impoundment differed from that of previous presidents, his perception of his constitutional authority also differed. This was an important factor in provoking the congressional response to impoundment in the 1974 Budget Act.

Notes

1. See *The Federalist Papers* (New York: The New American Library, 1961), no. 58, p. 359.

2. Art. I, Sec. 8.

3. Art. I, Sec. 9.

4. See Edward S. Corwin, *The President* (New York: New York University Press, 1957), p. 127.

5. "Prepared Statement of Hon. Joseph T. Sneed, Deputy Attorney General of the United States," U.S., Congress, Senate, Ad Hoc Subcommittee on Impoundment of Funds of the Committee on Government Operations and the Subcommittee on Separation of Powers of the Committee on the Judiciary, *Impoundment of Appropriated Funds by the President,* Joint Hearings on S. 373, 93d Cong., 1st sess., 1973 (hereinafter *1973 Hearings*), p. 364.

6. U.S., Congress, Senate, *Congressional Record,* 10 May 1973 (daily ed.), 119, S8872.

7. For a more complete treatment of these terms see Louis Fisher, analyst, *Budget Concepts and Terminology: The Appropriations Phase,* U.S., Library of Congress, Congressional Research Service, 21 November 1974, no. 74-210.

8. Congressional Budget and Impoundment Control Act of 1974, 88 Stat. 297.

9. His actions were declared illegal in Local 2186 A.F.G.E. v. Phillips, C.A., no. 371-73, 358 F. Supp. 60 (D.D.C. 1973).

10. 23 U.S.C. Sec. 101 et seq.

11. 86 Stat. 816.

12. Train v. New York City, C.A. no. 73-1377 (Feb. 18, 1975). For an analysis of litigation concerning impoundments in these stages of the budgetary process see Stuart Glass, analyst, *Presidential Impoundment of Congressionally Appropriated Funds: An Analysis of Recent Federal Court Decisions,* U.S., Library of Congress, 25 March 1974, no. 74-82A.

13. See, e.g., Berends v. Butz, 357 F. Supp. 143 (D. Minn. 1973); Local 2677 A.F.G.E. v. Phillips, C.A. no. 371-73, 358 F. Supp. 60 (D.D.C. 1973); Commonwealth of Pennsylvania v. Lynn, C.A. No. 990-73 (D.D.C., 23 July 1973).

14. See Joseph Cooper, "Analysis of Alleged 1803 Precedent for Impoundment Practice in Nixon Administration," in *1973 Hearings,* p. 676.

15. See Louis Fisher, "Impoundment of Funds: Uses and Abuses," *Buffalo Law Review* (Fall 1973), in U.S., Congress, Senate, *Congressional Record,* 4 February 1974 (daily ed.), p. S1165.

16. The first three stages are based on an analysis by Joseph Cooper. See statement by Joseph Cooper, U.S., Congress, Senate, Committee on the Judiciary, Subcommittee on Separation of Powers, *Executive Impoundment of Appropriated Funds,* Hearings, 92d Cong., 1st sess., March 1971 (hereinafter *1971 Hearings*), p. 181.

17. Mary Louise Ramsey, "Impoundment by the Executive Department of Funds which Congress Has Authorized it to Spend or Obligate," U.S., Library of Congress, Legislative Reference Service (1968), in *1971 Hearings,* pp. 291-92.

18. C.W. Dawes, *The First Year of the Budget of the United States,* (New York: Harper and Brothers, 1923), quoted in Cooper, *1971 Hearings,* p. 186.

19. Act of June 30, 1932, 47 Stat. 382.

20. Fritz Morstein Marx, "The Bureau of the Budget: Its Evolution and Present Role," Part 2, *American Political Science Review* 39 (1945):869.

21. Quoted in Cooper, *1971 Hearings,* p. 378.

22. J.D. Williams, "The Impounding of Funds by the Bureau of the Budget," The Inter-University Case Program, no. 28 (1955), in *1971 Hearings,* p. 380.

23. Nile Stanton, "History and Practice of Executive Impoundment of Appropriated Funds," *Nebraska Law Review* 53 (1974):10.

24. Public Law 71 (1942).

25. Williams, "The Impounding of Funds," *1971 Hearings,* p. 381.

26. Quoted in Ramsey Clark, "Federal-Aid Highway Act of 1956—

Power of the President to Impound Funds," *Opinions of the Attorney Generals* 42, no. 32 (1967), in *1971 Hearings*, p. 61.

27. Williams, "The Impounding of Funds," *1971 Hearings*, p. 386.

28. Ibid., p. 388.

29. Ibid., p. 389.

30. Fisher, "The Politics of Impounded Funds," *Administrative Science Quarterly* 15 (Sept. 1970):361, in *1971 Hearings*, p. 109.

31. Letter from President Truman to Secretary of Defense Johnson, in *1971 Hearings*, p. 525.

32. Ramsey, "Impoundment," *1971 Hearings*, p. 299.

33. Ibid., p. 300.

34. Louis Fisher has argued that this impoundment did not necessarily contravene congressional intent. See "Presidential Spending Discretion and Congressional Controls," *Law and Contemporary Problems* (Winter, 1972), in *1973 Hearings*, p. 683.

35. Fisher, "The Politics of Impounded Funds," *1971 Hearings*, p. 110.

36. See Hale Boggs, "Executive Impoundment of Congressionally Appropriated Funds," *University of Florida Law Review* 24:226.

37. The White House, "Precedents for Reserving Funds Appropriated by the Congress, But not Requested by the President," in *1971 Hearings*, p. 526.

38. Bureau of the Budget, "Memorandum to the President: Authority to Reduce Expenditures" (1961), in *1973 Hearings*, p. 338.

39. John H. Stassen, "Separation of Powers and the Uncommon Defense: the Case Against Impounding of Weapons System Appropriations," *The Georgetown Law Journal* 57 (1969):1159 at 1164.

40. U.S., Congress, House, Armed Services Committee, 87th Cong., 2d. sess., 1962, H. Rept. 1406, p. 9.

41. Ibid.

42. Ibid., pp. 5-7.

43. See Gerald W. Davis, "Congressional Power to Require Defense Expenditures," *Fordham Law Review* 44 (1964):39, in *1971 Hearings*, p. 569.

44. Theodore Sorenson, *Kennedy* (New York: Harper and Row, 1965), p. 348.

45. Letter from President Kennedy to Representative Carl Vinson, in *1971 Hearings*, p. 526.

46. Fisher, "Uses and Abuses," p. S1166.

47. Ramsey, "Impoundment," p. 502; Boggs, "Executive Im-

poundment," p. 226. President Kennedy's total impoundments by year are: 1961, $7.6 billion; 1962, $6.5 billion; 1963, $4.5 billion.

48. President Johnson's total impoundments by year are: 1964, $4.2 billion; 1965, $5.6 billion; 1966, $8.7 billion; 1967, $10.6 billion; 1968, $9.9 billion. Boggs, "Executive Impoundment," p. 226.

49. Stassen, "Separation of Powers," p. 1159 at 1169.

50. U.S., Congress, House, Armed Services Committee, 89th Cong., 2d sess., 1966, H. Rept. 1536, p. 2.

51. U.S., Congress, House, Armed Services Committee, 89th Cong., 2d sess., 1966, H. Rept. 1679, quoted in Stassen, "Separation of Powers," p. 1171.

52. Department of Defense Appropriations Act of 1968, Pub. Law No. 90-96, 81 Stat. 231.

53. U.S., Congress, House, Armed Services Committee, 90th Cong., 1st sess., 1967, H. Rept. 221, p. 8.

54. Clark, "Federal-Aid Highway Act," in *1971 Hearings*, p. 62.

55. State Highway Commission of Missouri v. Volpe, 479 F.2d 1099 (8th cir. 1973).

56. The White House, statement by President Johnson, 8 September 1966, in *1971 Hearings*, p. 527.

57. Fisher, "The Politics of Impounded Funds," *1971 Hearings*, p. 113.

58. Nile Stanton, "The Presidency and the Purse: Impoundment 1803-1973," *University of Colorado Law Review* (1973), in U.S., Congress, Senate, *Congressional Record*, 14 December 1973, p. S22925 at S22926.

59. Arthur M. Schlesinger, Jr., *The Imperial Presidency* (New York: Popular Library, 1974), pp. 232-33.

60. *Harvard Law Review* 86, no. 8 (June, 1973):1505 at 1511.

61. 23 U.S.C. Sec. 101 (c) (1970).

62. *Harvard Law Review* 86, no. 8 (June 1973):1512. The National Aquarium Project for Washington, D.C., was deferred by the Johnson administration and finally terminated by the Nixon administration.

63. 7 U.S.C. Sec. 901 (1970).

64. See Arnold and Porter Law Firm, "Memorandum to National Rural Electric Cooperative Association" (1973), in *1971 Hearings*, p. 594.

65. Fisher, "Uses and Abuses," p. S11678.

66. Stanton, "The Presidency and the Purse," p. S22926.

67. Fisher, "Uses and Abuses," p. S1167.

68. Quoted in ibid.

69. Ibid.

70. Louis Fisher, memorandum to Senator Ervin, in *1971 Hearings,* p. 595.

71. Fisher, "Presidential Spending Discretion," in *1973 Hearings,* p. 710.

72. *Weekly Compilation of Presidential Documents* 9, no. 5:109-10.

73. Fisher, "Uses and Abuses," p. S1163.

74. Quoted in "Protecting the Fisc: Executive Impoundment and Congressional Power," *Yale Law Journal* 82 (July 1973):1636.

4

The Legal and Constitutional
Basis for Impoundment

Members of President Nixon's administration made many legal and constitutional claims to justify his refusal to spend funds provided by Congress. They provided the only systematic defense of impoundment as a policy tool because the issue had not been a major source of friction between the president and Congress until the early 1970s.

The need for a legal analysis stems from the nature of constitutional government. The U.S. government is one of limited powers and each branch can only exercise those powers that have been provided in the Constitution. Of course, these powers have been modified and expanded by subsequent interpretation and practice, which are essential parts of the Constitution. The conclusion of this chapter is that none of the arguments proferred by administration officials is convincing. Nevertheless, it is important to take their arguments seriously and subject them to critical analysis.

The source of the impoundment controversy stems from the separation of powers system that delegates some powers to Congress and some to the presidency. The analysis begins with the premise that presidential impoundment, insofar as it contravenes the will of Congress, must be justified either by statute or by the Constitution. Since the "President's power, if any . . . must stem from an act of Congress or from the Constitution itself,"[1] the analysis examines possible statutory bases for impoundment and then moves to constitutional justifications.

First, consideration is given to the language in specific

statutes to see if there are general rules of interpretation that can be used to indicate congressional intent. Several authorization and appropriations measures are dealt with, but the problem is to discover how much discretion is inherent in congressional spending legislation. Presidents have argued that appropriations bills provide a broad range of discretion to the executive in expending (or not expending) the funds. Opponents of impoundment construe appropriations bills to circumscribe more narrowly the chief executive's discretion.

Second, more general statutory bases for impoundment are analyzed. Presidents have argued that some statutes, such as the Antideficiency Act or the Employment Act of 1946, give the executive branch a general authority to impound funds. They have argued, notwithstanding the provisions of specific appropriations bills, that since the president has the obligation to see that the laws are faithfully executed, it is his duty to choose from among conflicting statutes those that ought to be enforced. The authority of these general statutes was cited by President Nixon in claiming he was within the law, despite the seemingly mandatory nature of some specific spending measures.

The final and broadest type of justification considered is the president's powers and duties under the Constitution. The main argument against impoundment is that Congress has the power of the purse. If the chief executive can show that he shares enough in the fiscal power to refuse to spend appropriated funds, the will and intent of Congress are much less important. There can be no more appeal to statutes, and the president can contravene the will of Congress as he sees fit. The constitutional provisions cited to justify impoundment are the executive power provision and the commander in chief clause. These are examined to see if they can support the claim the executive branch has made.

The analysis proceeds from a narrower to a broader level of justification, with each higher level encompassing and superseding the lower levels. If specific spending measures do not allow impoundment, appeal is made to general statutes that can be read to supersede the specific laws. If these general statutes fail, appeal is made to the supreme law of the land, the Constitution.

Statutory Construction and the Nature
of Appropriations Measures

It is a general theory underlying the Constitution and the doctrine of separation of powers that Congress has the "power of the purse." That is, it shall make the basic decisions regarding the raising of revenues and their expenditure. It does so by passing authorization and appropriation laws, which the executive has the duty to faithfully carry out. The question examined here is the nature of the discretion that the executive has in carrying out spending laws. To what extent are appropriations mandatory and to what extent are they discretionary?

There is no contention that Congress cannot grant the president the authority to impound appropriated funds as it did in Title VI of the Civil Rights Act of 1964.[2] It is also accepted that Congress can condition the expenditure of funds and in many cases can compel their expenditures if it chooses.[3] There has been much contention, however, about the status of general appropriations bills. It is firmly established that authorization measures are not mandates to spend. As Representative Canon said: "All members of the House understand that the word 'authorize' as used in this connotation, means 'permitted'—and nothing more."[4] The status of appropriations measures, however, is not as clear.

In general, appropriations measures are not considered to be a mandate to spend all of the money appropriated. A classic statement of this is contained in a letter from Chairman of the House Appropriations Committee George H. Mahon to Senator Sam Ervin:

> It is, I believe, wholly accurate to say that, over the long span of time, through many Congresses and many administrations, the weight of experience and practice bears out the general proposition that an appropriation does not constitute a mandate to spend every dollar appropriated. That is a generally accepted concept. It squares with the rule of common sense. I subscribe fully to it.[5]

But he added that this ought not to have the effect of giving the president an absolute veto that was explicitly rejected by the constitutional convention. The common sense part of Mahon's statement refers to the fact that Congress appropriates money much in advance of the time it is actually to be spent. Thus it cannot possibly foresee all circumstances that might make spending the full amount undesirable.

To make this point, Attorney General Ramsey Clark, in an opinion supporting President Johnson's withholding of federal aid highway funds, quoted House Report 1797 (concerning the General Appropriations Act of 1951): "Appropriation of a given amount for a particular activity constitutes only a ceiling on the amount which should be expended for that activity."[6] However, he failed to quote the next sentence, which said: "The administration officials responsible for administration of an activity for which appropriation is made bear the final burden for rendering all necessary service with the smallest amount possible within the ceiling figure fixed by the Congress."[7] The full context indicates that appropriations measures constitute a legislative declaration of intent by the Congress that is binding on the president. Any discretion inherent in appropriations bills must be exercised within those limits. As the Court said in *Spaulding* v. *Douglas Aircraft Co.*: "The purpose of the appropriations, the terms and conditions under which said appropriations were made, is a matter solely in the hands of Congress and it is the plain and explicit duty of the executive branch of the government to comply with the same."[8] The presumption, then, seems to be that the executive is obliged to carry out the will of Congress, even if not all of the funds are expended.

William Rehnquist, then assistant attorney general, articulated a broad formulation in order to determine to what extent appropriations are mandatory. "In the question of trying to find a mandatory intent on the part of Congress, it is not a question of looking for the word 'shall' as opposed to 'may'." Congressional intent should be derived "from taking the overall language of the authorization bill, the enabling statute if there was one in the particular appropriations language, and construing them together to try to find on a reasonable basis what intent Congress manifested."[9]

Similar to Rehnquist's formulation, Mary Louise Ramsey, of the Library of Congress Legislative Reference Service, has concluded that Congress can mandate spending without using explicit language, such as "shall" or "directed." "Where Congress by substantive legislation, directs that a certain thing be done, and subsequently, by an appropriations bill, provides the funds for doing it, it can be argued that, taken together, the two measures constitute a mandate to spend so much of the appropriation as is necessary to give effect to the substantive law."[10]

Furthermore, the fact that Congress has at times granted presidents limited impoundment authority indicates that congressional intent in appropriations measures is not to grant wide discretion over expenditures. Also, to assume that Congress must explicitly define spending discretion in each appropriation act overlooks the fact that Congress has passed a general act defining the nature of discretion contained in appropriations acts: the Antideficiency Act Amendment of 1950.[11] Since this act spells out the conditions under which the withholding of appropriated funds is permissible, the burden of proof ought to be on the executive to show that a given case falls within those conditions. It can be concluded that, unless explicit authority is granted, the president may not rely on the general nature of appropriations acts to impound sums necessary to the execution of congressional intent.

General Statutory Bases for Impoundment

If the particular authorizing or appropriating legislation does not provide sufficient justification for the president to withhold funds, he may rest his actions on the authority of more general statutes dealing with the spending power. This section deals with the most important of such laws cited by the executive branch and examines the extent to which they provide the president with the authority to withhold funds.

The Antideficiency Act

In justifying impoundments Nixon administration officials relied heavily on the Antideficiency Acts of 1905 and 1906, as amended in 1950.[12] In a statement before a Senate subcommittee on impoundment of funds, Caspar W. Weinberger, deputy director of OMB, stated: "Perhaps the most explicit authority for withholding appropriated funds is section 3679 of the Revised Statutes—the so-called 'Antideficiency Act'."[13] In 1973 Roy Ash, director of OMB, stated before another hearing: "As we read under the Antideficiency Act, it does provide that if there are other developments subsequent to the date on which the appropriation was made available, that subjective judgments should be changed."[14]

The Antideficiency Act was formulated in 1905 in order to curtail the executive practice of coercive deficiencies, that is, the expenditure of all funds by a particular agency before the end of the fiscal year. This had the effect of forcing Congress to appropriate the additional funds or the agency would stop functioning. The act provided that department heads could apportion funds so that they would be released periodically throughout the fiscal year and not as a lump sum in the beginning.

Nevertheless, in the spring of 1947 the Post Office announced that, instead of apportioning its funds in equal amounts for each quarter, it had apportioned virtually all of its funds for the first three-quarters and would not have enough money to operate at the end of the year.[15] The Congress was thus faced with making supplemental appropriations or letting the Post Office stop operations. The Senate directed the Budget Bureau (BOB) and the General Accounting Office (GAO) to investigate the matter and see if there was a way the same situation could be avoided in the future. The BOB-GAO report concluded that deficiencies were impossible to avoid because changing conditions could not be forseen. But at the same time changing conditions might result in a surplus, which there was no incentive to conserve. The committee recommended enacting legislation to allow the reserving of savings to offset future deficits. But in setting aside such reserves, the report warned that the authority "must be exercised with considerable care in order to avoid usurping the power of Congress."[16] The Hoover Commission was appointed by President Truman in 1947 to examine federal management and problems of fiscal control. It advised that the president ought to be given authority to withhold funds once congressional intent was carried out.[17]

These recommendations were finally given legislative form in a rider (section 1211) to the General Appropriations Act of 1951. Subsection (c) of the act reads as follows: "In apportioning any appropriation, reserves may be established to provide for contingencies, or to effect savings whenever savings are made possible by or through changes in requirements, greater efficiency of operations, or other developments subsequent to the date on which such appropriation was made available." Therefore, reserves were to be established either (1) to provide for contingencies, or (2) to effect savings, but not to cancel or limit programs. The rest of subsection (c) reads:

> Whenever it is determined by an officer designated in subsection (d) of this section to make apportionments and reapportionments that any amounts so reserved will not be required to carry out the purposes of the appropriation concerned, he shall recommend the rescission of such amount in the manner provided in the Budget and Accounting Act, 1921, for estimates of appropriations.

Thus appropriations could be reserved, but only if the purpose of the legislation was carried out.

As has been noted, the above section was one of the main justifications for impoundments used by the Nixon administration. The main source of controversy was the nature of the "other developments" mentioned in the act. Administration officials gave this phrase an expansive reading, taking it to include inflation. This was the major reason for the Nixon impoundment of highway trust funds and water pollution control funds, two of the most significant Nixon impoundments. In order to determine the meaning of the section it is useful to examine the report of the House committee that wrote the law and subsequent interpretations of BOB and GAO.

The House committee that reported out the Omnibus Appropriation Act also issued a report of the type that is many times used to determine congressional intent. The report explained the need for section 1211 and further stated:

Appropriations of a given amount for a particular activity constitute only a ceiling upon the amount which should be expended for that activity. The administration officials responsible for administration of an activity for which appropriation is made bear the final burden for rendering all necessary service with the smallest amount possible within the ceiling figure fixed by the Congress.[18]

In reference to President Truman's refusal to expend the full amount of funds appropriated for the air force in 1949, the report said: "It is perfectly justifiable and proper for all possible economies to be effected and savings to be made, but there is no warrant or justification for the thwarting of a major policy of Congress by the impounding of funds."[19]

In construing the phrase "other developments" it would seem that the reference is to changes germane to individual programs and predicated upon the fulfillment of their purpose. It is a general tenet of statutory construction that the scope of catchall phrases such as "other developments" is limited by the prior terms of the passage. The prior terms in this case are "changes in requirements" and "greater efficiency of operations," which would seem to exclude different categories of developments, such as changes in the general economy.[20]

Finally, the act has been interpreted by authoritative government agencies. Analysis by OMB, of course, supported the president's broad reading of the act. However, the 1952 edition of the *Examiner's Handbook,* printed by BOB shortly after the act was passed, states: "Reserves must not be used to nullify the intent of Congress with respect to specific projects or level of programs."[21] The Government Accounting Office also has general duties of fiscal control. In response to a request from Senator Ervin's committee on impoundment in 1973, Elmer B. Staats, comptroller general, prepared an opinion stating:

There is abundant legislative history in connection with the enactment of the Antideficiency Act to support our conclusion that this legislation goes no further than authorizing the President to establish reserves to provide for contingencies, to reflect savings, and to take into account changes in requirements subsequent to the appropriation act, and to reserve funds because of changing circumstances. We are not aware of any specific authority which authorizes the president to withhold funds for general economic, fiscal, or policy reasons.[22]

Thus after examining the legislative history and the circumstances leading up to the 1950 amendment to the Antideficiency Act, the House report accompanying its enactment, general tenets of statutory construction, and various authoritative interpretations, it would seem that the act did not give the president authority to curtail programs significantly by impounding funds for reasons relating to the general economy. This particular justification for impoundment should not be a source of controversy in the future. In July 1974 President Nixon signed the Congressional Budget and Impoundment Control Act of 1974, Title X of which deletes the "other developments" clause from the Antideficiency Act.[23]

The Employment Act of 1946

The Employment Act of 1946 [24] was construed by the Nixon administration to confer a general discretion on presidents to modify appropriations measures in order to control inflation. Caspar Weinberger, deputy director of OMB, referred to it in his testimony before the Senate Judiciary Subcommittee on Separation of Powers on March 24, 1971.[25] Deputy Attorney General Sneed also relied upon it in his statement before Senator Ervin's hearings on impoundment in 1973.

The preamble to the act states that it is "the continuing policy and responsibility of the Federal Government to use all practicable means consistent with its needs and obligations and other essential considerations of national policy . . . to promote maximum employment, production, and purchasing power." The mention of purchasing power was taken to mean that the president must withhold funds in order to curb inflation, which would undercut purchasing power.[26]

An initial objection to that interpretation is that the act refers to the federal government and not to the president. Congress is also responsible for carrying out the purposes of the act and it is unlikely that it would delegate powers to the executive branch that could be used to oppose the will of Congress. The language cited by the administration is contained in the preamble to the act, while the rest of the act provides for a Joint Economic Committee in Congress, a Presidential Council of Economic Advisers, and an annual presidential report on the state of the economy. In construing statutes, however, the function of the preamble is to explain, not to grant any specific power.[27] In addition, it would be just as plausible to emphasize "maximum employment" rather than "purchasing power." In that case the act could be read to mandate more government spending on the theory that more spending would promote employment, production, and wages. Thus the language of the act gives no clear direction to the president to reduce spending by impounding funds.[28]

Spending and Debt Ceilings

Some of the justifications used by the Nixon administration for impounding funds are various statutory spending and debt ceilings. The argument was that the chief executive has the obligation to execute faithfully *all* of the laws, and when there is a conflict among them the president must use his judgment to decide which to execute. Consequently, when the full expenditure of all appropriations would violate a statutorily enacted ceiling, the president is obliged not to make the full expenditure. When Deputy Director of OMB Weinberger was testifying before the Senate Committee on Banking, Housing, and Urban Affairs, he stated: "The President may be confronted with specific limitations upon expenditures and he may from time to time be obliged to impose restrictions upon certain programs in order to insure that such limitations are not exceeded."[29]

Spending ceilings as a general grant of impoundment authority are considered first. There was no contention that spending ceilings, which explicitly give the president authority to cut funds at his discretion, are invalid. But when passing general spending ceilings, Congress has shown a consistent desire to keep spending discretion in its own hands. For example, the 1969 spending ceiling explicitly provided that Congress could appropriate more funds if it chose.[30] And in 1970 the House Appropriations Committee stated:

the committee in initiating an all-encompassing ceiling last year, was not seeking to advance a vehicle for arbitrary broad-axe type cutbacks that would leave to the Executive the allocation of any spending reduction to specific agencies and programs. The whole idea was to focus on the totality of Federal Spending by putting control of *total* spending in the hands of Congress, adjustable *only* by the Congress.[31]

Given the fact that in passing a spending ceiling Congress sometimes specifically gives the president authority to cut some spending,[32] it seems that spending ceilings without such a provision do not grant to the president a general power to impound.

In fiscal 1958 the Eisenhower administration announced that it would implement a series of cutbacks and stretchouts in order to stay within the statutory debt limit. When the debt ceiling was raised, the funds were released.[33] The Nixon administration also used the debt ceiling as a justification for impoundment. Deputy Attorney General Sneed stated: "When appropriations exceed the federal government's revenues, the President may be obliged to impound appropriations in order to comply with the debt limit."[34]

Statutory debt ceilings are enacted until the end of fiscal years, at which time they are reviewable by Congress. In fiscal 1973 the Nixon administration impounded $3.4 billion in order to stay below the $465 billion debt ceiling.[35] However, much of the money impounded was for construction and contract authority, which probably could not have been expended before the end of fiscal 1973 when the debt ceiling would be reviewed. In addition, whenever the national debt has threatened to pierce the ceiling, Congress has consistently raised the ceiling.[36] Thus in reality the administration was impounding in order to keep below a ceiling that Congress might pass for the next fiscal year. So there was only an attenuated possibility of conflict between statutes that the president had to reconcile.

In view of the fact that Congress refused to give the president impoundment power in H.R. 16810 (1972), it is doubtful that it intended to let the president replace congressional priorities with executive ones through the statutory debt limit. However one feels about the general desirability of holding down the national debt, it must be admitted that the national debt limit is not a sound basis upon which to base impoundment.

The Economic Stabilization Act of 1970

The Nixon administration also cited the Economic Stabilization Act of 1970 in support of its assertion of the right to impound. Deputy Attorney General Sneed told a Senate committee on February 6, 1973, that "the President has substantial latitude to refuse to spend or to defer spending for general fiscal reasons, such as the control of inflation."[37] He then referred to the Economic Stabilization Act Amendments of 1971[38] to support his statement. This act allows the president to control prices, rents, wages, salaries, dividends, and interest rates in order to stabilize the economy.[39] Controlling government spending is not one of the powers enumerated, so Congress presumably did not want to include it. Also since the procedures of the act are set up to place controls on the private sector of the economy, they have no relationship to impoundment.[40]

It is clear that Congress did not intend the Economic Stabilization Act to be used to grant authority for impoundment. On February 19, 1973, just thirteen days after Sneed's testimony, Senator Eagleton introduced an amendment to the act. It provided that nothing in the act "may be construed to authorize or require the withholding or reservation of any obligational authority provided by law, or of any funds appropriated under such authority."[41] The amendment was enacted into law when the Economic Stabilization Act was extended on April 30, 1973.

The Constitutional Basis for Impoundment

If the president fails to find authority for his refusal to spend in individual statutes or in the more general laws just examined, he is forced to fall back on his constitutional powers as president. This section will consider the constitutional justifications that have been put forward to justify presidential refusal to spend appropriated funds. It begins with the general doctrine of separation of powers. It then examines arguments stemming from the executive power clause, including the claims of inherent power and historical precedent as legal justification. The section concludes with a consideration of the commander-in-chief power and how it cuts across the impoundment question.

Separation of Powers

The broadest constitutional argument that can be made for the president's authority to impound funds is the somewhat vague doctrine of separation of powers. The doctrine is nowhere specifically stated in the Constitution. The doctrine is taken to be implied by the opening sections of the first three articles of the Constitution. The legislative power is to be vested in a Congress, the executive power in a president, and the judicial power in one Supreme Court and inferior courts established by Congress.

Although Congress makes the laws, their execution is left to the executive; this includes the actual expenditure of funds. So the president cannot be entirely excluded from fiscal control. Corwin holds that there are two constitutional areas in which the power of the Congress and that of the president blend: one is the area of foreign affairs and defense, and the other is that of spending.[42] Thus it has been argued that drastically curbing the president's impounding power (or practice) would convert the chief executive into a "chief clerk."[43]

A case is made here for general congressional efficacy; that is, if a necessary power is not explicitly delegated to either the president or Congress, when there is a clash of wills, the will of Congress ought to prevail.[44] The case for the efficacy of specific authorization and appropriations measures has already been made, and the executive power and commander in chief arguments are examined later.

The strongest argument for congressional efficacy is the "plain meaning" of the constitutional provision that the executive shall "take Care that the Laws be faithfully executed."[45] The Supreme Court has construed this provision several times in favor of Congress' will. In *Kendall* v. *United*

States ex rel Stokes[46] the Court had to decide whether President Jackson's postmaster general had to pay a person who had contracted, under law, to carry the mails. In deciding for the plaintiff, the Court held that "to contend that the obligation imposed on the President to see the laws faithfully executed, implies a power to forbid their execution, is a novel construction of the Constitution and entirely inadmissible."[47] Similarly, Justice Black, in deciding that President Truman did not have the authority to seize the steel mills in 1952, declared: "The Constitution limits [the president's] functions in the lawmaking process to the recommending of laws he thinks wise and the vetoing of laws he thinks bad. And the Constitution is neither silent nor equivocal about who shall make laws which the President shall execute."[48]

An argument more specifically referring to the spending process was made by President Wilson in a message to Congress in 1920. "The Congress has the power and the right to grant or deny an appropriation, or to enact or refuse to enact a law; but once an appropriation is made or a law passed, the appropriation should be administered or the law executed by the executive branch of the Government."[49] Justice Rehnquist, at the time he was Assistant Attorney General, argued that the president has no authority to impound funds for domestic purposes. He concluded that "it seems an anomalous proposition that because the executive branch is bound to execute the laws, it is free to decline to execute them."[50]

Another argument for congressional efficacy is based on the presence of the veto provision in the Constitution.[51] In the first place, the president's refusal to spend certain monies appropriated in a bill would amount to an item veto. The item veto appeared in the provisional constitution of the Confederate States of America and since then has been almost exclusively a product of the states. There is no evidence that the framers ever considered such a provision. Although proposals to confer on the president the power of item veto with respect to appropriations measures have been introduced often, Congress has never enacted such a measure by proposing an amendment or by legislative action.[52]

Secondly, the power to impound funds might amount to an

absolute veto, which the framers specifically rejected.[53] This would be the case if the president refused to spend funds, even if Congress provided them by overriding his veto, as happened with water pollution control funds in fiscal 1973. Corwin takes the position that once the veto power has been exercised, the president must comply with Congress' will.

> he was endowed by the Constitution with a qualified veto upon acts of Congress with the idea in mind among others that he might thus protect his prerogatives from legislative curtail-ment. But this power being exercised, this power of self-defense is at an end; and once a statute has been duly enacted, whether over his protest or with his approval, he must promote its enforcement by all the powers constitutionally at his dis-posal.[54]

The Executive Power

Article II of the Constitution begins, "The executive Power shall be vested in a President of the United States of America." From this clause arises the argument that the president has the constitutional authority to impound funds, which is implicit in the fact that he is the chief executive. Presidential defenders have argued that the executive power clause is not merely a summary description of the office but rather a positive grant of comprehensive executive power.[55] In support of this interpreta-tion, the Justice Department quotes Alexander Hamilton: "The general doctrine of our Constitution then is, that the *executive power* of the nation is vested in the President; subject only to the *exceptions* and *qualifications,* which are expressed in the instrument."[56] This argument is in the vein of Theodore Roosevelt's stewardship theory of the powers of the office that holds that the president can exercise powers that are not explicitly forbidden by the Constitution.

Caspar Weinberger, testifying for the Nixon administration in 1971, argued that the power to withhold appropriated funds is implicit in Article II of the Constitution.[57] Joseph T. Sneed, as deputy attorney general, argued that the executive power includes the duty to administer the national budget, which implies a duty to avoid fiscal instability.[58] Since Congress may spend more money than the president feels is proper for the health of the economy, he may have to impound funds to protect the fiscal integrity of the nation. Director of OMB Roy Ash, in testimony before a Senate committee, stated: "The detailed administration of projects, the negotiating and letting of contracts, the identification of payees and determination of their eligibility for payment, and the essential exercise of judgment in the normal conduct of Government operations— all of these, by their very nature, are clearly executive functions."[59] The question is whether the nature of executive power, as interpreted above, can justify the refusal of the president to expend funds that Congress wishes spent. The case of presidential-congressional disagreement is posited here because if the president had congressional approval or statutory authority, there would be no need to appeal to the Constitution.

Inherent power. The question of inherent power has been dealt with by the Supreme Court and several cases are usually cited as authority.[60] *In re Neagle* was an 1890 case that involved the appointment by the attorney general of a deputy marshal to protect Justice Field while he was riding circuit in California. In protecting the justice, Neagle killed a man and was arrested for murder by local authorities. In habeas corpus proceedings the question arose over the authority of the president to appoint Neagle. The Supreme Court held that the president did have such authority and that the duties of the executive are not limited to the enforcement of acts of Congress or treaties according to their express terms, but include duties "growing out of the Constitution itself, our international relations and all the protection implied by the nature of the government under the Constitution."[61] This rather broad language, however, is undercut by the Court's concurrent reliance on certain statutes that would also cover the situation. This brings into doubt the use of *Neagle* as a strong precedent for the existence of inherent powers in the executive branch.[62]

In re Debs[63] is also cited by proponents of the inherent power theory. That case involved the validity of an injunction against strike activities that would obstruct the mails. The Supreme Court sustained the injunction and spoke of broad national powers "to remove all obstructions upon highways, natural or artificial, to the passage of interstate commerce," and of the right of the executive to appeal to the courts.[64] This case was also undercut as a clear exposition of inherent power because of the mention of a supporting congressional act in the last paragraph.[65] Furthermore, the case seems to involve the inherent power of the federal government rather than the inherent power of the president, but the Court ratified the action of the presidency and the judiciary acting together. Impoundment involves the presidency acting in opposition to the will of Congress.

One of the most extensive treatments of inherent executive power is found in *Youngstown Sheet & Tube Co.* v. *Sawyer*.[66] In that case the Supreme Court decided that President Truman had overstepped his bounds in seizing the steel mills in order to prevent a strike. The president argued that he had the inherent power to do so because of the crisis created by the Korean War. The Court ruled that such an act was a legislative function and, as such, could not be performed by the president. It is pointed out, however, that there was no majority opinion and that Justices Jackson and Clark, though voting with the majority, believed that inherent powers might exist in some situations. In so far as inherent powers are considered to exist, however, they seem to exist in situations of emergency when direct action is needed. Although inflation and fiscal integrity are significant problems, it is doubtful that they are emergencies of such a nature as to trigger the inherent power doctrine.

The steel seizure case makes a strong argument against the inherent power theory as used to justify impoundment of funds. Despite the existence of the relationship of the president's action to his duties as commander in chief, inherent power was found not to exist. In addition, Justice Jackson's opinion framed presidential-congressional conflicts in terms relevant to the impoundment problem:

When the President takes measures incompatible with the expressed or implied will of Congress, his power is at its lowest ebb, for then he can rely only upon his own constitutional powers minus any constitutional powers of Congress over the matter. Courts can sustain exclusive presidential control in such a case only by disabling the Congress from acting upon the subject.[67]

Claiming an inherent presidential power to refuse to spend congressionally appropriated funds is difficult in the face of such a formulation.

The argument for inherent presidential power is often intermingled with the argument for the existence of inherent power in the federal government. In order to apply to the impoundment controversy, there has to be an assertion of inherent presidential power superseding that of Congress in the area of federal spending. *Neagle* and *Debs* do not make that case, and *Youngstown* militates strongly against it. As Assistant Attorney General Rehnquist argued:

> It is in our view extremely difficult to formulate a constitutional theory to justify a refusal by the President to comply with a Congressional directive to spend. It may be argued that the spending of money is inherently an executive function, but the execution of any law is, by definition, an executive function, and it seems an anomalous proposition that because the Executive branch is bound to execute the laws, it is free to decline to execute them.[68]

The justification of presidential actions by historical precedent, that is, because other presidents have done the same thing, is part of the inherent power argument, and is now considered.

Historical precedent. The Nixon administration in defending its impoundment policies has argued that impoundment was a long accepted historical practice. In testimony before Senator Ervin's impoundment hearings on February 6, 1973, Joseph T. Sneed, deputy attorney general, said: "Such a long-continued executive practice, in which Congress has generally acquiesced, carried with it a strong presumption of legality."[69] Elsewhere he has stated: "In my judgment, the warrant of historic practice is perhaps the strongest support for my position."[70] The argument that historical precedent constitutes legal justification for a practice is part of the position that the executive power includes other implied powers. What other presidents have done defines, in part, those implied powers.

The most frequently quoted decision in making the historical precedent argument is *U.S.* v. *Midwest Oil Co.*[71] At issue was the validity of a presidential order by President Taft in 1908, withdrawing from further sale to private individuals certain public oil lands in California. This was contrary to an act of Congress that stated that the lands were to remain available to the public. The government argued that the president's action was taken in the public interest with tacit congressional approval. The Court found that 282 similar withdrawals had occurred over the past fifty years, and that since Congress had acquiesced, President Taft had the inherent power to make the withdrawal. Justice Lamar wrote for the majority: "Government is a practical affair intended for practical men . . . unauthorized acts would not have been allowed to be so often repeated as to crystalize into a regular practice."[72]

The steel seizure case presented similar claims. The Justice Department had cited other instances in which presidents had seized private business enterprises in order to settle labor disputes. Justice Black, writing for the Court, rejected the argument: "But even if this is true, Congress has not thereby lost its exclusive constitutional authority to make laws." Justice Frankfurter, while concurring with the Court, stated the case for historical precedent as legal justification:

> In short, a systematic, unbroken, executive practice, long pursued to the knowledge of the Congress and never before questioned, engaged in by Presidents who have also sworn to uphold the Constitution, making as it were such exercise of power part of the structure of our government, may be treated as a gloss on "executive power" vested in the President by section 1 of Article II.[73]

Frankfurter's argument that historical usage creates constitutional authority is not persuasive in the impoundment case. Impoundment has never been sanctioned by the courts or by Congress. Congress has passed laws that allow the president to withhold funds in specific and limited ways, but what is at question here is impoundment without such legislative sanction. The historical precedent argument can be undermined in three ways. First, not all previous impoundments have gone unchallenged. Second, only President Nixon has made a sweeping claim to the power. Third, President Nixon used impoundment in ways different from all previous presidents.

One of the main elements of Frankfurter's formulation of the historical precedent argument is that the practice be "long pursued to the knowledge of the Congress and never before questioned."[74] It is true that Congress has in the past given the president the explicit authority to impound for specific purposes and periods of time. Such impoundments, however, are not in dispute. On other occasions in the past, members of Congress have spoken out against presidential withholding of funds. The first major controversy between Congress and the presidency occurred in 1942 when President Roosevelt began to withhold funds from projects not considered essential to the national defense.[75] This resulted in Senator McKellar's two antiimpoundment legislative riders, although neither survived intact.[76] Major impoundment disputes also erupted during the administrations of Truman, Eisenhower, and Kennedy. Therefore, it cannot be said that the Congress supinely accepted a systematic and unbroken string of executive impoundments.

It may also be relevant to the claim of executive prerogative to impound funds that other presidents have made the same claim, aside from their actions. Such claims have seldom been made. In illustration of the contrast between the role conception of the modern Office of Management and Budget and the Bureau of the Budget just after it was formed in 1921 is the following statement by Charles Dawes, in his book on the first year of BOB:

> we have nothing to do with policy. Much as we love the President, if Congress in its omnipotence over appropriations and in accordance with its authority over policy, passed a law that garbage should be put on the White House steps, it would

be our regrettable duty, as a bureau, in an impartial, non-political, and nonpartisan way to advise the Executive and Congress as to how the largest amount of garbage could be spread in the most expeditious and economical manner.[77]

Such a role conception was certainly not reflected in statements about executive control of the budget by the Nixon administration.

Franklin Roosevelt did claim authority to impound funds but his claim was explicitly limited by the intent of Congress.[78] President Kennedy expressed some doubts about the legality of impoundment. When the Civil Rights Commission proposed that he cut off government funds going to institutions practicing racial discrimination, he said: "I don't have the power to cut off the aid in a general way, . . . and I think it would probably be unwise to give the President of the United States that kind of power."[79] President Johnson asserted the power to impound funds for reasons of economic stability, and President Nixon has made a sweeping constitutional claim to impoundment authority.[80] As the above illustrates, there has not been a unanimous consensus among presidents that they possess the authority to impound funds.

Finally, even if it is conceded that past actions without legitimation from Congress or the courts would justify present impoundments, President Nixon's impoundments can be distinguished from those cited as precedent. As has been explained in the previous chapter, President Nixon made several significant departures from precedent in his impoundment policy, besides impounding greater sums. He impounded nonmilitary funds in the face of previous expressions of congressional intent to the contrary,[81] he terminated entire programs by the withholding of all funds,[82] and he cut off funds for programs not requested in his proposed budget.[83] Thus when historical precedent is used as justification, care must be taken to assure that the precedent cited is of the same type as the action being justified.

The historical precedent argument for impoundment has been examined from three angles: types of impoundments, congressional reaction, and presidential claims to the power.

There remains some doubt as to whether the precedents are so "systematic," the Congress so acquiescing, and presidents so consistent in claiming the authority as to constitute the "gloss on 'executive power'" of which Justice Frankfurter spoke.[84] As Justice Miller said in affirming a Court of Claims decision: "It may also be questioned whether the frequent exercise of a power unauthorized by law, by officers of the government, can ever by its frequency be made to stand as a just foundation for the very authority which is thus assumed."[85]

Commander in Chief

In Corwin's analysis the two areas of the Constitution in which the power of the president and that of the Congress blend are those of foreign affairs and spending.[86] The problem of impoundment in the area of foreign affairs and defense is thus doubly complicated. This area of impoundment is generally recognized to be a special case and will be treated as such. No attempt will be made to examine the broader aspects of congressional and presidential prerogatives in foreign affairs. The problem here is: in spite of a lack of authority to impound in a given instance, does the commander-in-chief clause justify the use of impoundment, if that instance concerns national defense?

The framers purposefully split the military power of the United States between Congress and the president. Neither could control the military apparatus without the other. Congress had the power to mobilize national resources in raising an army and navy, but the president as commander in chief could command the armed forces. Before 1940 policy conflicts between president and Congress over defense were infrequent. But after 1940 with the increasing importance of defense, particularly the large portion of the national budget consumed by it, Congress has come to play a greater role in defense policy making.[87]

The authority of the president as commander in chief is somewhat unclear because Article II, Section 3, confers an office rather than specifying a function. As Justice Jackson said: "These cryptic words . . . imply something more than an empty title. But just what authority goes with the name has plagued presidential advisors who would not wave or narrow it by nonassertion yet cannot say where it begins or ends."[88] Presidential spokesmen, however, have claimed that the commander-in-chief clause does confer on the president the authority to impound funds for defense purposes.

Caspar Weinberger in testimony before a Senate committee in 1971 said: "As far as the President's power as Commander in Chief is concerned, I think that there is a good legal argument . . . that the overriding powers that have to go with the Commander in Chief's authority are such that they may well be in a separate category and that the powers incident to that authority are not subject to other powers or limitations in the Constitution."[89] Assistant Attorney General Rehnquist, who argued that the president does not have authority to impound funds in domestic matters, held that the area of foreign affairs is special and that the president may impound in such cases.[90] Deputy Attorney General Sneed in 1973 also argued that "the President has substantial authority in the areas of national defense and foreign relations,"[91] including the power to impound funds.

One of the bases for these arguments is the historical precedent argument—that other presidents have also done so. It is true that presidents since Franklin Roosevelt have asserted impounding authority in the area of defense. However, the same general objections that were put forth above to the more general historical precedent are also applicable here.

The main constitutional authority cited in this area is *U.S.* v. *Curtis-Wright Export Corp.*[92] The case involved the right of the president to prohibit arms sales to a country pursuant to a joint resolution of Congress. The Supreme Court upheld that right and Justice Sutherland went on to paint a very broad picture of presidential prerogatives in foreign affairs. There has been some disagreement as to how much of the opinion constitutes obiter dicta,[93] but the case has been used as a strong precedent for presidential power in foreign affairs. The question is, does this power also reach the budgetary process?

Youngstown had drawn the line at the edge of the domestic arena. The acquisition of weapons systems, as opposed to their deployment, has important implications for our foreign policy, but such acquisitions are handled through the ordinary budgetary process. In order to justify impoundment, the links between defense and the domestic process involved have to be quite direct, as indicated by *Youngstown*. Justice Jackson's opinion is to the point here:

> The Constitution expressly places in Congress power "to raise and support armies" and "to provide and maintain a Navy." This certainly lays upon Congress primary responsibility for supplying the armed forces. Congress alone controls the raising of revenues and their appropriation and may determine in what manner and by what means they shall be spent for military and naval procurement.[94]

Notes

1. Youngstown Sheet & Tube Co. v. Sawyer, 343 U.S. 579, 585 (1952).

2. See Arthur S. Miller, "Presidential Power to Impound Appropriated Funds—An Exercise in Constitutional Decision-Making," *North Carolina Law Review* 43 (1965):50-2, in *1971 Hearings,* p. 315.

3. See Spaulding v. Douglas Aircraft Co., 60 F. Supp. 985, 988, affirmed, 154 F.2d 419 (1946). But cf. Rehnquist testimony, U.S., Congress, Senate, Committee on the Judiciary, Subcommittee on Separation of Powers, *Executive Impoundment of Appropriated Funds,* Hearings, 92d Cong., 1st sess., 1971 (hereinafter *1971 Hearings*), p. 235. Although President Harding thought Congress could not compel spending, see Edward S. Corwin, *The President* (New York: New York University Press, 1957), p. 398. President Kennedy's campaign to have Chairman Vinson change the language from mandatory to discretionary on the RS-70 authorization bill indicates that he felt the Congress could direct him to spend funds. President Nixon vetoed some bills, in part because he felt they provided more money than he thought it wise to spend. Among them were the Water Pollution Control Act of 1972 and the Hospital Construction Bill. See Frank Church, "Impoundment of Appropriated Funds: the Decline of Congressional Control over Executive Discretion," *Stanford Law Review* 22 (1970):1240, in *1971 Hearings,* pp. 364, 372. If he felt he had complete discretion not to spend funds,

the amount of the money appropriated would have no bearing on whether he vetoed the bill or not.

4. Quoted in Gerald W. Davis, "Congressional Power to Require Defense Expenditures," *Fordham Law Review* 44 (1964):39, in *1971 Hearings,* p. 596.

5. Letter from George H. Mahon to Senator Ervin, in *1971 Hearings,* p. 501.

6. Ramsey Clark, "Federal-Aid Highway Act of 1956—Power of President to Impound Funds," *Opinions of the Attorney Generals* 42, no. 32 (1967), in *1971 Hearings,* p. 61.

7. U.S., Congress, House, Appropriations Committee, General Appropriations Act of 1951, 81st Cong., 2d sess., 1951, H. Rept. 1797, p. 9.

8. 60 F. Supp. 985, 988, affirmed 154 F.2d 419 (1946).

9. *1971 Hearings,* p. 234.

10. Mary Louise Ramsey, "Impoundment by the Executive Department of Funds which Congress Has Authorized It to Spend or Obligate," U.S., Library of Congress, Legislative Reference Service (1968), in *1971 Hearings,* pp. 291, 298.

11. 31 U.S.C. Sec. 665 (1970).

12. A.D. Act 1905 ch. 1484, Sec. 4, 33 Stat. 1257, as amended 31 U.S.C. Sec. 665 (1970).

13. *1971 Hearings,* p. 95; see also p. 149.

14. U.S., Congress, Senate, Ad Hoc Subcommittee on Impoundment of Funds of the Government Operations Committee and the Subcommittee on Separation of Powers of the Committee on the Judiciary, *Impoundment of Appropriated Funds by the President,* Joint Hearings on S. 373, 93rd Cong., 1st sess., 1973 (hereinafter *1973 Hearings*), p. 286.

15. Louis Fisher, "Anti-Deficiency Act," in *1973 Hearings,* p. 398.

16. BOB-GAO Report, *1973 Hearings,* p. 398.

17. J. D. Williams, "The Impounding of Funds by the Bureau of the Budget," *The Inter-University Case Program,* no. 28 (1955), in *1971 Hearings,* pp. 378, 392.

18. U.S., Congress, House Appropriations Committee, General Appropriations Act of 1951, 81st Cong., 2d sess., 1951, H. Rept. 1797, p. 9.

19. Ibid., p. 311.

20. "Impoundment of Funds," *Harvard Law Review* 86 (June 1973):1517.

21. Quoted in Williams, "The Impounding," p. 393.

22. *1973 Hearings,* p. 102.

23. U.S., Congress, House, *Congressional Record,* 11 June 1974 (daily ed.), pp. H4979, H4999.

24. 15 U.S.C. Sec. 1021 (1970).

25. *1971 Hearings,* p. 96.

26. Louis Fisher, "Impoundment of Funds: Uses and Abuses," *Buffalo Law Review* (Fall 1973), in U.S., Congress, Senate, *Congressional Record,* 4 February 1974 (daily ed.), pp. S1162, S1164.

27. "Presidential Impoundment: Constitutional Theories and Political Realities," *Georgetown Law Journal* 61: 1296, 1303 n. 70.

28. In Hearings before Senator Ervin's subcommittee in 1971, Professor Arthur S. Miller said to Deputy Director of OMB Weinberger: "I find it incredible, if I may say so, that you would rely on the Employment Act of 1946. This is beyond belief." *1971 Hearings,* p. 153.

29. Quoted in Louis Fisher, "Presidential Impoundment of Funds," U.S., Library of Congress, Congressional Research Service, in *1971 Hearings,* pp. 594-5. See also Weinberger testimony, *1971 Hearings,* p. 96; and Ash statement *1973 Hearings,* p. 270.

30. "Presidential Impoundment," *Georgetown Law Journal,* p. 1304 n. 71.

31. U.S., Congress, House, Appropriations Committee, 91st Cong., 2d sess., 1970, H. Rept. 1033, p. 95.

32. As it did in 1967 and 1968. See Fisher, "The Politics of Impounded Funds," *Administrative Science Quarterly* 15 (Sept. 1970):361, in *1971 Hearings,* pp. 103, 113-14.

33. Fisher, "Uses and Abuses," p. S1164.

34. *1973 Hearings,* p. 366. See also Ash statement, p. 270.

35. "Impoundment of Funds," *Harvard Law Review,* p. 1520.

36. Ibid., p. 1522. See also Senator Chiles statement in *1973 Hearings,* p. 377.

37. Fisher, "Uses and Abuses," p. S1164.

38. P.L. 92-210.

39. "Impoundment of Funds," *Harvard Law Review,* p. 1519.

40. Ibid.

41. Quoted in Fisher, "Uses and Abuses," p. S1164.

42. Corwin, *The President,* p. 127.

43. Statement of Deputy Attorney General Sneed, *1973 Hearings,* pp. 364, 369.

44. The following discussion is based on the general argument set forth in the "The Likely Law of Executive Impoundment," *Iowa Law Review* 59 (1973): pp. 50, 70-74.

45. Art. II, Sec. 3.

46. 37 U.S. (12 Pet.) 524 (1838).

47. Ibid., p. 613.

48. Youngstown Sheet & Tube Co. v. Sawyer, 343 U.S. 579, 587 (1952).

49. Quoted in Davis, "Congressional Power," *1971 Hearings,* p. 578.

50. Memorandum, "Re Presidential Authority to Impound Funds Appropriated for Assistance to Federally Impacted Schools," in *1971 Hearings,* pp. 279, 283.

51. Art. I, Sec. 7.

52. See statement by the Comptroller General, "The Antideficiency Act," in *1973 Hearings,* pp. 110-14.

53. Sally Weinraub, "The Impoundment Question—An Overview" *Brooklyn Law Review* 40 (Fall 1973):347.

54. Corwin, *The President,* p. 66.

55. Justice Department, *1973 Hearings,* p. 893.

56. Ibid.

57. *1971 Hearings,* pp. 134-41.

58. *1973 Hearings,* p. 369.

59. Ibid., p. 270.

60. Justice Department, *1973 Hearings,* p. 839.

61. 135 U.S. 1, 67 (1890).

62. Robert E. Goosetree, "The Power of the President to Impound Appropriated Funds; With Special Reference to Grants-in-Aid to Segregated Activities," *The American University Law Review* 11 (1962):32, in *1971 Hearings,* p. 590.

63. 158 U.S. 564 (1895).

64. Ibid., p. 599.

65. Ibid., p. 600. Also Goosetree, "The Power," *1971 Hearings,* p. 590.

66. 343 U.S. 579 (1952).

67. Ibid., p. 637-38.

68. *1971 Hearings,* p. 283.

69. Statement in *1973 Hearings,* p. 359.

70. Justice Department, *1973 Hearings,* p. 842.

71. 236 U.S. 459 (1915). Also see Corwin, *The President,* p. 120.

72. 236 U.S. 459 (1915). It has been argued that there was an element of emergency in the Midwest Oil case and that lands were being claimed so quickly that President Taft had to act before Congress could change the law. His order was issued "in aid of proposed legislation." See "Protecting the Fisc: Executive Impound-

ment and Congressional Power," *Yale Law Journal* 82 (July 1973): 1636 n. 53.

73. 343 U.S. 579 (1952), pp. 610-11.

74. Ibid.

75. Ramsey, "Impoundment," *1971 Hearings*, p. 293.

76. Williams, "The Impounding," *1971 Hearings*, pp. 388-89.

77. *The First Year of the Budget of the United States* (New York: Harper and Brothers, 1923), in Joseph Cooper, "Executive Impoundment of Appropriations," *1971 Hearings*, pp. 181, 186.

78. Ramsey Clark, letter to secretary of transportation, *1973 Hearings*, pp. 872, 875.

79. Quoted in "Protecting the Fisc," *Yale Law Journal*, p. 1645 n. 61.

80. Andrew J. Glass, "Congress weighs normal procedures to overturn Nixon impoundment policy," *National Journal* 5 (17 February 1973):236.

81. "Impoundment of Funds," *Harvard Law Review*, p. 1511.

82. Ibid., p. 1512.

83. Fisher, "Presidential Spending Discretion and Congressional Controls," *Law and Contemporary Problems* (Winter 1972), in *1973 Hearings*, pp. 683, 710.

84. Youngstown Sheet & Tube Co. v. Sawyer, 343 U.S. 579 (1952), pp. 610-11.

85. The Floyd Acceptances, 74 U.S. (7 Wall) 666, 667 (1969).

86. Corwin, *The President*, p. 127.

87. John H. Stassen, "Separation of Powers and the Uncommon Defense: the Case Against Impounding of Weapons System Appropriations," *The Georgetown Law Journal* 57 (1969):1159, 1162.

88. Youngstown Sheet & Tube Co. v. Sawyer, 343 U.S. 579, 641 (1952).

89. *1971 Hearings*, p. 144.

90. Ibid., p. 325.

91. Statement in *1973 Hearings*, p. 368.

92. 299 U.S. 304 (1936). See Justice Department, *1973 Hearings*, p. 834. See also Rehnquist testimony in *1971 Hearings*, p. 248.

93. See the Bickel-Rehnquist exchange, *1971 Hearings*, p. 248.

94. 343 U.S. 579, 643 (1952).

5

The Judiciary Enters
the Budgetary Process

Beginning in 1971 the district courts began to decide cases that challenged the impoundment actions taken by President Nixon. This entrance of the courts into the budgetary process was a departure from precedent, but it was in accord with recent trends of judicial activism. The adjudication of impoundment cases by the courts is an important aspect of the whole controversy. In addition to the resolution of particular disputes, court decisions provided added legitimation to congressional assertions that the president was impinging on its power of the purse.

This chapter deals with the role of the courts in this interbranch dispute over the spending power. The first concern is to put into perspective the decision of the judiciary to enter the political process. In addition to the broad historical trends, there were specific demands from the political system influencing the judiciary to accept impoundment cases for resolution. Once such cases had been accepted, the courts operated under a set of internal institutional constraints that tended to channel the outcomes in certain directions. After these factors have been examined, the chapter focuses on the appeals process and the Supreme Court's decision in the consolidated water pollution control cases.

The Role of the Judiciary in the Political Process

The Constitution provides that the judicial power of the United States shall extend to all cases and controversies arising under the Constitution. Although the Constitution created a system of checks and balances with a separation of powers framework, the Supreme Court largely defines its own powers. Even though "each department should be able to defend its characteristic functions from intrusion by either of the other departments,"[1] the Supreme Court has assumed the power of judicial review. Ever since John Marshall asserted in *Marbury v. Madison* that "It is emphatically the province and duty of the judicial department to say what the law is,"[2] the Supreme Court has been the final arbiter in disputes over constitutional rights and prerogatives.

This is not to say that the Court has always used its power. In addition to the formal limits to its jurisdiction stated in the Constitution, it has followed various norms of self-restraint. This reluctance to use its asserted power stems from practical as well as ideological considerations. In a tactical sense it would be foolish for the Court to make rulings that would probably be ignored and that it could not enforce. Ideologically, the Court has been very self-conscious of its appointed status in an electoral democracy, as well as the narrow scope of the judicial forum.

In a concurring opinion in *Ashwander* v. *TVA*[3] Justice Brandeis set forth some general rules the Court would observe in making constitutional decisions. The Court will only rule on a constitutional issue if there is no way to avoid it. If the issue can be put off, decided on statutory ground, or if there is a way to construe a statute as valid, the Court will avoid the constitutional issue. These rules of judicial self-restraint are subject to varying interpretations by different justices. They do, however, provide some general parameters for the judicial function, and give the Court a rationale for avoiding certain decisions.

Since Congress is the popular branch, the Court has hesitated to strike down laws as unconstitutional—although it has done so on important occasions, such as some New Deal legislation. In the past the Court has tended to uphold (or at least not to rule against) presidential actions, again with some notable exceptions. "While the Court has sometimes rebuffed presidential pretensions, it has more often labored to rationalize them; but most of all it has sought on one pretext or other to keep its sickle out of this 'dread field'."[4] Accordingly, in *Mississippi* v. *Johnson* the Court refused to restrain President Andrew Johnson from carrying out an alledgedly unconstitutional law. "An attempt on the part of the judicial department of the government to enforce the performance of such duties by the President might be justly characterized, in the language of Chief Justice Marshall, as 'an absurd and excessive extravagance'."[5] In *Myers* v. *U.S.*[6] the Court overturned a law that required the consent of the Senate before the president could dismiss certain executive officers appointed by him.[7] In the area of foreign affairs the Court has recognized the special needs and abilities of the executive branch. A strong statement of this defense is found in *U.S.* v. *Curtiss-Wright Export Corp.*[8]

More generally, the expression of judicial self-restraint with regard to the other two branches is contained in the doctrine of political questions. This doctrine, which is primarily a function of separation of powers, was reviewed by Justice Brennan in *Baker* v. *Carr.*[9] Among the criteria for political questions that he listed were: a textually demonstrable commitment of an issue to another branch, a lack of judicial standards for resolving the issue, or possible embarrassment to the other branches if the Court's decision differed from theirs. Thus the Supreme Court has a ready-made excuse, if it considers a dispute between the other two branches too politically volatile.

Despite the formal and informal limits to the Court's power, over the last two centuries it has steadily expanded the scope of its power. In the area of foreign affairs it delivered a major blow to the asserted primacy of the president in the steel seizure case.[10] In question was the president's seizure of the steel mills for purposes of national security—despite specific procedures Congress had provided for such a situation, which did not include seizure. Also the Court has struck down treaty agreements that violated the constitutional rights of U.S. citizens.

The issue of reapportionment had been avoided by the Supreme Court for several decades despite litigation challenging existing electoral boundaries. In 1962 the Court ruled in

Baker v. *Carr*[11] that reapportionment was not a political question and that there were sufficient judicial standards to decide such cases. The decision led to increased judicial involvement in the drawing of electoral boundaries.

The Court has also recently been more willing to make decisions that directly impinge on the other two branches. The Constitution provides that "each House shall be the Judge of the . . . qualifications of its own Members."[12] This seems close to a "textually demonstrable constitutional commitment" to the Congress to decide who its own members are. Yet in *Powell* v. *McCormack*[13] the Court ruled that the denial of a seat to Adam Clayton Powell constituted an *exclusion* of an elected member. Such an exclusion could not be made, although the *expelling* of a member might be acceptable under Art. I, Sec. 5, cl. 2, once the member has been seated. This distinction allowed the Court to get around the political questions doctrine in interpreting the Constitution "in a manner at variance with the construction given the document by another branch."[14]

The Burger Court, despite the presence of four Nixon appointees, was willing to decide against the executive branch. In *U.S.* v. *U.S. District Court*[15] the Supreme Court upheld a lower court decision that certain wiretaps authorized by the attorney general and justified on national security grounds were in violation of the Fourth Amendment. In *U.S.* v. *Washington Post Co.*[16] the Court refused to enjoin the publication of the Pentagon Papers. The Burger Court also dealt a blow to assertions of executive prerogative in its ruling on the doctrine of executive privilege.[17] While recognizing the necessity of some form of executive privilege the Court rejected the absolute claim of President Nixon to withhold any information when he deemed it to be in the national interest to do so. The doctrine of separation of powers played heavily in the opinion but was insufficient to support the "absolute, unqualified presidential privilege of immunity from judicial process under all circumstances."[18]

From this brief survey it can be seen that the courts have shown an increasing willingness to decide important political issues, some of which affect directly the constitutional powers and prerogatives of the other two branches. Justice Frankfurter, no advocate of judicial activism, said in the steel seizure case: "The judiciary may, as this case proves, have to intervene in determining where the authority lies as between the democratic forces in our scheme of government."[19] Learned Hand has argued that, although judicial review is not necessarily implied in the structure of the Constitution, it is a necessary condition for its successful operation. There has to be an arbiter when disagreements arise or each branch will go its own way and the system will break down.[20] Justice Jackson wrote that "Some arbiter is almost indispensible when power . . . is balanced between different branches, as the legislative and executive. . . . Each unit cannot be left to judge the limits of its own power."[21] This willingness of the judiciary to insert itself into the political process upon appropriate occasions was reasserted by Chief Justice Burger in *U.S.* v. *Nixon* in denying the president's claim of absolute privilege of confidentiality for all presidential communications: "Many decisions of this Court, however, have unequivocally reaffirmed the holding of *Marbury* v. *Madison* that 'it is emphatically the province and duty of the judicial department to say what the law is'."[22]

The judicial response to impoundment litigation since 1971 fits into the above pattern of increasing judicial activism in the political process. Although in one of the first impoundment cases a district court dismissed the case on the grounds that there was no authority for the proposition "that a United States District Court may compel the head of the Executive Branch of government to take any action whatsoever,"[23] virtually all of the subsequent impoundment cases have been allowed in court. The procedural barriers of unconsented suits against the sovereign and political questions have been easily overcome. The vast majority of the cases have also been decided against the government on the merits and judges have been willing to compel appropriate executive action.

In attempting to understand judicial policymaking in the impoundment area it is necessary to consider both external and internal determinants of judicial decision making. The initial decision to adjudicate can be seen largely in terms of external demands on the courts originating in the political system.

Once the cases are accepted, outcomes can be seen in the light of internal institutional constraints on judicial policymaking. The categories, of course, are not mutually exclusive, but provide a convenient analytic distinction. External factors will be considered first.

External Factors Affecting the Courts

Ever since the presidency of Franklin Roosevelt the executive branch has been impounding appropriated funds, many times resulting in cries of outrage from the Congress.[24] This was partially a function of whose ox was being gored, but it was accompanied by the rhetoric of separation of powers and constitutional prerogatives.[25] Hearings were held and anti-impoundment legislation was introduced, though never successfully passed. It was clearly a dispute between the two branches, though not a dominating issue. An interesting question is why the issue was not presented to the courts for resolution until 1971.

Part of the answer may lie in the partisan array of political forces in 1971. Leaving aside for the moment the military-related impoundments because of their peculiar legal status, previous large scale domestic impoundments have occurred only under Presidents Franklin Roosevelt and Lyndon Johnson, both Democrats dealing with Democratic Congresses.[26] Neither the nature of their impoundments nor their partisan political situations were comparable to the Nixon impoundments. President Nixon was a Republican president who was actively and explicitly trying to change the policy priorities of the Johnson administration and its legislative program. This put his impoundments into the context of an acute partisan battle, and may have provoked the resort to the judicial forum.

Closely connected with the priority-changing substance of the Nixon impoundments was the style of the president. Rather than trying to soft-pedal his differences with the Congress, President Nixon asserted constitutional prerogatives that seemed to be a threat to the traditional congressional grasp on the purse strings. More threatening than the actual slipping of the purse strings from congressional hands, which had been occurring for most of this century, was the formal and symbolic assertion of constitutional rights by President Nixon: "The constitutional right of the President of the United States to impound funds, and that is not to spend money, when the spending of money would mean either increasing prices or increasing taxes for all the people—that right is absolutely clear."[27]

In addition to the style and rhetoric of the Nixon impoundments, there were also changes in the substance of impoundment policy. He impounded funds prospectively, eliminated entire programs, and impounded despite explicit congressional expressions of intent to the contrary (in nonmilitary areas).[28] Most of the impoundments were in the area of domestic Democratic priorities. These exercises of impoundment practices were a significant departure from the actions of previous presidents. The sharp escalation of the quality and quantity of impoundments during the Nixon administration gave impetus to the search for a judicial solution.

Not all of the funds that were impounded reverted to the treasury. Many were unimpounded by "fine tuning," that is, by gradually releasing impounded funds in order to alleviate political complaints.[29] This process could be used to reward friends and punish political enemies.[30] Consequently, the executive branch as an institution acted in systematic ways that resulted in the denial of funds to certain individuals and groups who, as a result, brought cases to court to claim what they argued was rightfully theirs. In response to such litigation U.S. district courts began to accept impoundment cases for adjudication.

Litigants were not the only ones to respond to executive impoundment actions. Congress, as an institution, felt threatened. There were increasingly frequent cries of alarm directed at the president and his alleged usurpation of the congressional spending power. At the same time that these cries were being heard, however, Congress was unable to pass a general antiimpoundment bill, though several were introduced. Part of the reason for this was congressional ambivalence over federal spending. It wanted expenditures cut but it did not want the president to decide where. There was also the feeling that, since the issue was being litigated, the pressure for an immediate legislative remedy was lessened. The Supreme Court decision on the issue, however, did not come until after the passage of the Congressional Budget and Impoundment Control Act of 1974.[31]

Scholars have noted that "recent history suggests that legislative inaction is an important determinant of input demands on the Court (as, for example, in reapportionment and civil rights questions.)"[32] The refusal of the Congress to pass antiimpoundment legislation until the summer of 1974 constitutes such an input demand on the courts to settle impoundment disputes. Inaction is not the only way Congress influenced the judicial decision to accept impoundment litigation. Members of Congress also submitted an amicus curiae brief in the Missouri highway trust fund case, and Congressman Fred B. Rooney sued in court for funds as a member of Congress.[33]

Internal Constraints upon the Courts

Once the courts have accepted a series of cases it cannot be assumed that external factors are of no importance. This chapter argues, however, that internal institutional constraints are of primary importance in the resolution of the impound-ment cases. The judiciary is characterized by a set of general constraints limiting the way in which it can make policy. These can be divided into procedural and substantive considerations (the merits) discussed in full below. Impound-ment decisions have indicated important directions in these areas that will influence future adjudication, not merely the resolution of impoundment cases.

In addition, the courts operate under a range of other internal constraints, including the doctrines of judicial self-restraint and political questions, already mentioned. They also feel bound by the intent of the framers in constitutional litigation and legislative intent in cases of statutory construc-tion. Appellate courts are not bound by decisions in the lower courts, nor are lower courts bound by the decisions of other courts at their level. The weight of judicial opinion, however, may be a factor, and the virtual unanimity of court decisions in impoundment litigation may have influenced the Supreme Court decision.

One of the major constraints on judicial decision making is the norm of conforming to precedent. But there was no clear precedent to follow in the impoundment cases. Lower court judges, however, were nearly unanimous in their disposition of impoundment cases, deciding against the administration virtually all of the time. Social background research on judges is based on data from cases in which judges disagree and makes the inference that personal values are converted into judicial policy outputs. But given the near unanimity of decisions against the government in this highly controversial area, institutional constraints take on added importance as determinants of judicial decisions.

The major procedural and substantive issues in the impoundment litigation viewed as internal institutional constraints on judicial decision making will now be discussed. First, the issues are considered separately, illustrating the judicial response with representative examples from the many cases. There is a more detailed discussion of each issue as it is involved in the consolidated water pollution control cases, since the Supreme Court chose these cases to decide.

Some of the most important litigation in the impoundment controversy has arisen from the refusal of the Nixon administration to allot funds provided in the Federal Water Pollution Control Act Amendments of 1972.[34] The act was to provide $24.6 billion for the purpose of significantly improving the quality of the nation's waters by 1983 and eliminating pollutant discharges by 1985. The Environmental Protection Agency (EPA) was empowered to let out matching grants to states and municipalities of $5 billion in fiscal 1973 and $6 billion in fiscal 1974 for the construction of pollution abatement plants.

In the fall of 1972 Congress and the president were engaged in a battle over spending priorities, the president seeking to cut expenditures in accordance with his best judgment. In October

Congress voted to increase the national debt by $15 billion, raising it to $465 billion. In passing the bill the House also approved a spending ceiling of $250 billion for fiscal 1973 that would have given President Nixon unilateral authority to cut federal programs and activities in order to preserve the ceiling. The Senate, however, was unwilling to give the president total discretion over spending priorities and specified limits to the cuts that could be made. This was not acceptable to the White House and, as a result, there was no spending ceiling included in the legislation.[35]

Immediately upon hearing of the failure to pass the $250 billion ceiling, President Nixon vetoed the Federal Water Pollution Control Act.[36] In his veto message President Nixon stated: "Certain provisions of S. 2770 confer a measure of spending discretion and flexibility upon the President, and if forced to administer this legislation I mean to use those provisions to put the brakes on budget-wrecking expenditures as much as possible."[37] Nixon's main objection to the act was that it provided too much money whose expenditure would cause unacceptable inflationary pressures. After consideration of the president's objections, however, Congress overrode his veto by votes of 52-12 in the Senate and 247-23 in the House.

As he had indicated, the president proceeded to limit expenditures pursuant to the act despite the congressional override of his veto. He directed EPA Director William D. Ruckelshaus not to allot the full amounts authorized. On November 28, 1972, the EPA stated that in accordance with the president's instructions it was allotting to the states in fiscal years 1973 and 1974 "sums not to exceed $2 billion and $3 billion, respectively," instead of the $5 billion and $6 billion required by the act.[38] The administration argued that such actions were within its discretion in executing the law. Opponents, however, have charged that the funds were illegally and unconstitutionally impounded.

In order to understand the legal issues involved, it is necessary to understand the procedures for spending funds set up by the act. In the past, federal aid to localities for construction of sewage treatment plants was handled according to the usual procedure of authorization and then appropriation. This had the drawback of creating uncertainty on the part of local governments as to how much funding they would receive until appropriations were finally made, which were usually considerably less than authorizations. This made it difficult to plan and enter into contracts at the local level.

In order to remedy this situation the Federal Water Pollution Control Act set up a mechanism known as "contract authority" so that the ultimate grantees would know ahead of time the amounts that would be available for expenditure. According to the procedures set up by the act there were a series of steps which constituted funding.

1. Funds were authorized to be appropriated (Sec. 207).
2. Funds were allotted to the states according to a formula (Sec. 205).
3. Localities submitted proposals for water treatment facilities that were reviewed by the EPA and approved if the plans were adequate [Sec. 203, 201(g)(2), and 204].
4. The federal share of the funds for a project were obligated by the administrator. At this time local governments could enter into contracts with the firms that would construct the facilities [Sec. 203 and 201(g)(1)].
5. Congress appropriated the money to pay the construction firms as the payments fell due.
6. Funds were actually disbursed [Sec. 203(b) and (c)].

The focus of most of the litigation under this act was on the second step because the EPA had refused to allot the funds that the administration intended not to spend. One case, however, is based on the actual refusal to obligate the funds (steps four, five, and six). Before the merits of a case can be reached, there are a series of procedural requirements unique to the judiciary that must be fulfilled. These threshold questions will be dealt with before the substantive question of the language of the act and congressional intent are considered.

Procedural Constraints

The procedural constituents of internal institutional constraints on the judiciary are jurisdiction and justiciability. Before a court *can* consider a case, the matter must fall within the jurisdiction of the court. That is, the court must have the legal authority to decide the question. Elements of jurisdiction are: the proper forum, standing, and sovereign immunity, that is, the prohibition against unconsented suits against the sovereign. Before a court *will* hear a case, it must be convinced that the matter is justiciable. Aspects of justiciability include ripeness and the doctrine of political questions.

The proper forum. Cases can get into the federal district courts if there is a federal question involved or if there is diversity of citizenship between the parties. Impoundment cases are usually suits against federal administrators in Washington, D.C. Thus both conditions are usually fulfilled.

The Constitution gives Congress the power to "constitute tribunals inferior to the Supreme Court,"[39] and to regulate the jurisdiction of the Supreme Court.[40] Plaintiffs in impoundment cases have used several statutes pursuant to these provisions to gain access to the federal courts. The Mandamus Act provides that "the district courts shall have original jurisdiction of any action in the nature of a mandamus to compel an officer or employee of the United States or any agency thereof to perform a duty owed to the Plaintiff."[41]

Once jurisdiction of the courts had been established under this act, it ceased to play an important role in the impoundment litigation.[42] Another statute frequently used to enter the federal forum is the Federal Question Statute.[43] It provides that district courts shall have original jurisdiction in all civil actions in which the amount in controversy exceeds the value of $10,000. Such a requirement was easy to meet in impoundment cases, most of which involved substantially larger sums. The Declaratory Judgment Act does not confer jurisdiction by itself, but can be used in conjunction with jurisdictional statutes.

In 1973 the State of Georgia sought to invoke the original jurisdiction of the Supreme Court in an impoundment case involving several different federal programs. The Court, however, declined to accept the case on October 9, 1973.

Standing. Article III of the Constitution provides that the judicial power of the United States shall extend to cases and controversies. If a party can show it is suffering actual harm that it has a legal right to protect, the party has standing to sue in court. The party must allege "such a personal stake in the outcome of the controversy as to assure that concrete adverseness which sharpens the presentation of issues upon which the Court so largely depends."[44] There must also be demonstrated a "logical nexus between the status [of the plaintiff] asserted and the claim sought to be adjudicated."[45]

In one of the impoundment cases it was ruled that the plaintiff did not have standing to sue. In *Brown* v. *Ruckelshaus* consolidated with *City of Los Angeles* v. *Ruckelshaus*,[46] Judge Hauk ruled that the plaintiffs failed to produce evidence demonstrating that EPA's refusal to allot funds would cause them injury. When legislation has been set up to disburse funds to certain classes of persons or agencies upon the approval of certain requirements, the statutory beneficiaries have generally been granted standing to sue.[47] States have been granted standing when they allege that they qualify for funds for which they have submitted applications under the provisions of a specific act.

A union of government employees was held to have standing when it alleged that its members' jobs were threatened by the threatened dismantling of OEO. In *Local 2677 A.F.G.E.* v. *Phillips*[48] Judge W. B. Jones enjoined the defendant from continuing to dismantle OEO and terminating funding of Community Action Agencies before the end of the fiscal year.

In the water pollution control cases, standing was granted to a variety of parties. The injury asserted by all of the parties involved the poor condition of water that would be ameliorated if the EPA made all of the funds available to the states. The right asserted is that Congress passed legislation that legally entitled states to funds authorized under that act. Sec. 505(a) of the act also states that "any citizen may commence a civil action on his own behalf . . . (2) against the administrator when there is alleged a failure of the administrator to perform any act or duty under this Act which is not discretionary with the Administrator." There must, however, be a demonstration of the injury alleged.

States and municipalities are in a position to assert such an injury, but injury is not assumed merely from the withholding of funds. In *Minnesota* v. *Fri*[49] the state submitted affidavits showing that there were a large number of applications for grants pending that could not be filled under the present lack of funds but that might be funded if Minnesota's full share of the funds were made available. (The City of New York showed that it had two waste treatment projects that were approved by the EPA which it could begin but not complete because of the reduced allotments allowed after impoundments.) This "resulted in serious planning delays that will necessarily retard the development of sewage treatment facilities."[50]

In *Campaign Clean Water, Inc.* v. *Ruckelshaus,*[51] the plaintiff consisted of an association of individuals asserting economic and recreational interests in clean waters in Virginia. They demonstrated pecuniary injury resulting from waste contamination of Virginia's waters. "Such injury is particularized and sets these members apart from the public, in general."[52] In *Anthony R. Martin-Tricona* v. *Ruckelshaus*[53] a private citizen appearing in a pro se capacity had standing. He asserted his use of Lake Michigan for personal recreation purposes and his use of water services of the city, which used Lake Michigan as a source, as grounds for the suit.

Standing is not automatic, however. In *Brown* v. *Ruckelshaus*[54] Judge Hauk dismissed a water pollution control impoundment suit for lack of standing. It was a combined suit by the City of Los Angeles and Congressman George E. Brown, Jr., against the EPA to force the release of funds provided in the act. The court ruled that the plaintiffs failed to show that EPA's refusal to allot the full authorized sums was injuring them or would do so in the future. Specifically, they failed to produce any affidavits showing that any pollution control projects had been rejected because of frozen funds.

The court also noted that Brown's status as a congressman did not place him in any better position regarding standing than any other member of the general public. That was not the final word on the standing of congressmen, however. In July 1974 Judge June Green ruled[55] that Congressman Fred B. Rooney had standing to challenge the impoundment of funds under the Basic Water and Sewer Facilities Grant Program.[56] The total "reserving" of all funds appropriated for the program effectively "nullified his vote as a member of Congress and substantially affected his ability to represent his constituents."[57]

Parties alleging injury as a result of impoundments were able to take advantage of Rule 23(a) of the Federal Rules of Civil Procedure to bring class action suits against the government.[58] The ability of plaintiffs to bring class action suits, however, was circumscribed by recent decisions that required that every member of a class action suit brought in federal court must meet the $10,000 requirement without aggregating them.[59] Also "Individual notice must be sent to all class members whose names and addresses may be ascertained through reasonable effort."[60] The Court also ruled that petitioners had to bear the burden of the cost of notification.[61]

Sovereign immunity. One of the main objections brought by the Justice Department in these cases was the bar against unconsented suits against the sovereign. Under the doctrine of sovereign immunity, the United States is immune to suits unless it consents to be sued.[62] Two general exceptions to the doctrine are the Tucker Act,[63] through which the government can be sued in contract, and the Tort Claims Act of 1946, permitting suits in tort. There are also many specific statutes that allow citizens to sue the government.

The government argued that a suit, although nominally against an officer of the government, is in reality a suit against the United States if "the judgment sought would expend itself on the public treasury or domain, or interfere with the public administration,"[64] or "if the effect of a judgment would be to restrain the government from acting or to compel it to act."[65] Although the first two impoundment cases denied relief because of sovereign immunity,[66] no subsequent suits were dismissed for that cause.

One way the doctrine was circumvented in the water pollution control cases was that most of the plaintiffs asked only that funds be allotted (step 2), not that they actually be obligated or expended (steps 4, 5, and 6). This put those cases outside the *Land* v. *Dollar* rule barring forced expenditures.

The other vehicle used to avoid the sovereign immunity doctrine was the major exception provided in *Dugan* v. *Rank.*[67] This ground was relied upon exclusively in *Campaign Clean Water, Inc.* v. *Ruckelshaus,*[68] which sought obligation as well as allottment of impounded funds. According to *Ex Parte Young*[69] a suit can be brought against a government official who has failed to perform official duties. In *Dugan* the Court ruled that a suit can be brought against an officer of the government if the suit alleges that the officer exceeded statutory authority or acted within authority premised upon a power that is unconstitutional. The water pollution impoundment cases all allege that EPA exceeded its statutory authority in its refusal to allot or release the funds. *Campaign Clean Water, Inc.* thus fell squarely within the *Dugan* exception to the sovereign immunity doctrine.

Plaintiffs also argue that the Administrative Procedures Act (APA)[70] effectively waived sovereign immunity. Section 10(a) of the act states that a person "adversely affected or aggrieved by agency action . . . is entitled to judicial review thereof." Section 10(e) empowers federal courts to "compel agency action unlawfully withheld or unreasonably delayed" and to "hold unlawful and set aside agency action . . . not in accordance with law." The circuits are split as to whether the APA constitutes a blanket waiver of sovereign immunity, but the claim of the impoundment challengers was that they were "adversely affected" by agency action and that immunity was waived in such cases.[71] Finally, the challengers contended that Sec. 505 (a)(2) of the Water Pollution Control Act (quoted on p. 000) explicitly waived sovereign immunity for this act.

Ripeness. While the rules of jurisdiction have to do with the legal authority of the courts, the rules of justiciability are concerned with prudence and self-restraint. The line between the two concepts is blurred, but the former is more likely to be a matter of established law and the latter is more likely to be a matter of sound judicial and political judgment. The aspects of justiciability involved in the water pollution control impoundment cases are ripeness and the doctrine of political questions (discussed below). For either of these reasons a court may decide not to hear a case even though there is no question that it has formal jurisdiction.

The issue of ripeness is concerned with the proper timing of the litigation rather than the genuine nature of the injury alleged. If an issue is brought before the court too soon there may not yet be an actual controversy, that is, a premature case may be hypothetical. Or the issue may not yet be ready for judicial resolution. For instance, a challenge to a decision of a federal agency will not be ripe for judicial resolution until all administrative remedies have been exhausted.

Ripeness was an issue in *Missouri* v. *Volpe*[72] where the question of a declaratory judgment for future fiscal years was being considered. The Court ruled that such a judgment would be appropriate if the same type of illegal conduct might be expected to occur again in the future. In *Local 2677 A.F.G.E.* v. *Phillips*[73] the Court held that even though funds for Community Action Programs under OEO would not be entirely terminated until the end of the fiscal year, the suit was ripe because notices of termination had sufficiently interrupted the ongoing activities of the agencies.

In the water pollution control cases the issue of ripeness was intertwined with the special funding procedures set up under the act. The government argued that antiimpoundment suits brought under the Water Pollution Control Act were premature in that actual funds had not yet been denied.[74] Yet according to the spending procedures set up by the act, money must first be allotted before it can be spent. Funds are provided on a yearly basis, and those available funds that are not allotted in the appropriate year lapse and revert to the general treasury. If, however, funds for a given year are allotted but are not obligated, they remain available for obligation in future fiscal years.

The main reason for setting up this sort of a spending procedure was to enable states and cities to engage in long-range planning, a necessity in developing costly water treatment systems.[75] Since unallotted funds will lapse at the end of each fiscal year,[76] the courts considered suits to compel allotment to be "ripe, pressing and hotly in dispute,"[77] and thus not hypothetical and premature.

Political questions. The doctrine of political quesitons is a maxim of judicial self-restraint whose classic exposition was by Justice Brennan in *Baker* v. *Carr*. He argued that "The nonjusticiability of political questions is primarily a function of the separation of powers." He then set forth the criteria by which one might judge matters to be political questions or not. They are:

> a textually demonstrable constitutional commitment of the issue to a coordinate political department; or a lack of judicially discoverable and manageable standards for resolving it; or the impossibility of deciding without an initial policy determination of a kind clearly for nonjudicial discretion; or the impossibility of a court's undertaking independent resolution without expressing lack of the respect due coordinate branches of government; or an unusual need for unquestioning adherence to a political decision already made; or the potentiality of embarrassment from multifarious pronouncements by various departments on one question.[78]

Brennan then emphasized that the doctrine is one of "political questions" not "political cases." In other words, the doctrine does not exclude politically contentious issues, but only (and not all) those involving a separation of powers or other issues inappropriate for judicial resolution. Raoul Berger, however, has argued that the political questions doctrine "was self denying judicial construct without roots in constitutional history."[79]

Judge Carter in *San Francisco Redevelopment Agency* v. *Nixon*[80] held that a suit to compel the president to carry out a law passed by Congress was not appropriate for the Court. He said that not since *Marbury* v. *Madison* had the courts even contemplated compelling the president to take any action whatsoever. Other courts, however, have seen the issue as one of a ministerial duty of the president that does not involve his executive duties. Thus judgments do not breach the separation of powers and are within the traditional duties of the judiciary. In *Commonwealth of Pennsylvania* v. *Lynn* Judge Richey held:

> The issues in this case, however, concern the power of the Secretary to act under statutory programs already passed by Congress, and his power to act under the Constitution. Clearly

it is within the province of the judicial branch to determine the nature of the Congressional mandate and whether the Defendants have refused to comply with that mandate. This case does not present a nonjusticiable political question.[81]

The government argued that the water pollution impoundment cases presented political questions that were thus not justiciable. It argued that, while spending controls are not textually committed to the president or Congress, it is clearly not a matter for the judiciary. It further argued that Article II comes close to committing the spending responsibility to the president.

Instead of confronting the larger issue of congressional versus presidential prerogatives in federal spending, the courts have chosen to consider the narrower issue of statutory interpretation. They have chosen to decide the question of whether the administration ought to perform what was alleged by plaintiffs to be a purely ministerial duty.[82] Judge Merhige held that "to support the defendant's contention would require the Court to postulate a broad reading of executive power which includes the proposition that the Congress may make funds available for spending or mandate the manner in which they are spent, but may not mandate that they, in fact, be spent."[83]

The other political questions criterion that the government cited was a "lack of judicially discoverable and manageable standards for resolving" the question. The courts have also rejected this contention as a mischaracterization of the issue before the court. Statutory interpretation is a traditional function of the courts; they were asked to determine whether a ministerial act was commanded by a statute or not. Excessive involvement in agency affairs was not contemplated. "The Court is not being asked to supervise the operations of the EPA. Solely sought here is declaratory and injunctive relief with respect to the announced policy of impoundment."[84]

Substantive Constraints

When the threshold and procedural questions have been settled and it has been determined that there is an actual case or controversy and the court has jurisdiction, the court may proceed to the merits, or substance, of the issue. Unlike Congress, the courts may focus only on the specific legal issues involved with the parties to the suit at bar. They may not judge the overall wisdom of the policies in question, but must confine their decisions to the narrow legal questions presented in the case. This is not to assert that courts always do this, but merely that it is a widely accepted judicial norm.

The substantive question in the impoundment cases was whether the executive could legally stop expenditure of funds at certain stages in the administrative process. Some legislative programs have been set up in the form of a two-stage appropriations process in which funds are first allotted among the states according to a statutory formula.[85] Then proposals for expenditure are submitted by the states and, if approved by the administrator, the funds are actually obligated to be spent. Such a program was set up in the Federal Aid Highway Act of 1956[86] and the Federal Water Pollution Control Act Amendments of 1972.[87] In carrying out the latter act the administrator refused to allot 55 percent of the funds among the states in order to curb inflation. This refusal to allot is one way to accomplish the impoundment of funds.

The executive branch also interrupted the spending process at the second stage of the two-stage process by allotting funds, but then refusing to approve state submitted plans. Such was the case when the Department of Transportation refused to release highway trust funds to states that had complied in all respects with the requirements for funding under the act. In *State Highway Commission of Missouri* v. *Volpe*[88] the court held that the act did not give to the administrator the discretion to base spending decisions on criteria other than those found within the act itself. The status of the national economy was not one of those criteria. Campaign Clean Water, Inc., made a similar argument to the Supreme Court in its suit to obtain funds under the Water Pollution Control Act. It argued that the refusal to commit 55 percent of the funds appropriated constituted an abuse of discretion.[89]

A third type of spending control practiced by the Nixon administration was the refusal to accept and process applications for grants submitted by potential recipients. In most cases litigated, the court held that administrators may turn down specific applications that do not meet the statutory criteria, but the refusal to accept or process any applications is not allowed by the statute setting up the program.[90]

In the water pollution control cases the substantive question was whether or not the administrator of the EPA had the authority, at the President's discretion, to refuse to release to the states 55 percent of the funds provided in the Water Pollution Control Act. Specifically, the controversy centered around Sections 205(a) and 207 of the act,[91] which provided for allotment and authorization of the funds. The question was whether or not those two sections granted to the executive discretion to withhold the funds. There are two avenues of approach to the problem of determining legislative intent. One is the analysis of the "plain meaning" of the words. If that fails to produce a definitive answer, the legislative history of the act and its passage may be examined. The lower courts have utilized both avenues in these cases.

Section 205(a) of the Water Pollution Control Act provides that "Sums authorized to be appropriated pursuant to section 207 for each fiscal year . . . shall be allotted by the Administrator."[92] Section 207 reads "There is authorized to be appropriated to carry out this title . . . for the fiscal year ending June 20, 1973, not to exceed $5,000,000,000, for the fiscal year ending June 30, 1974, not to exceed $6,000,000,000."[93] The question was whether or not the language in these two sections granted to the administrator the discretion to withhold 55 percent of the funds. With one exception, all of the plaintiffs in the district courts argued that the word "shall" in section 205(a) meant that the administrator must allot all funds available. Any discretion granted to the administrator must be exercised at the obligation stage. Campaign Clean Water, Inc., however, conceded discretion at the allotment stage, but claimed that the withholding of 55 percent of the funds by the EPA constituted an abuse of discretion.

Prominent in the argument of the government was the fact that the bill was amended in conference to delete the word "all" which appeared before "sums" in Section 205(a), and the insertion of "not to exceed" before each of the sums mentioned in Section 207. The government contended that these changes indicated the intent of Congress to give the administrator discretion not to spend all of the funds authorized. There seems to be two questions; one relates to allotment and the other to obligation. The district courts were not unanimous in their rulings.

The combination of the phrases "shall allot" and "not to exceed" in the act seemed to indicate different meanings. As Judge Gasch stated in *City of New York* v. *Ruckelshaus*, "a 'plain meaning' analysis is obviously inadequate to the task at hand."[94] In such a case it becomes important to examine the legislative history of the act, particularly the expressions of intent by the sponsors of the bill. Particularly important, and most often quoted in opinions, were the statements of Representative Harsha, the Republican manager of the bill in the House and member of the conference committee, and those of Senator Muskie, manager of the bill in the Senate and member of the conference committee.

The plaintiff states emphasized the strong intent of Congress to commit significant national resources to the improvement of the condition of the nation's waters. There was much congressional debate over the amount of funds to be provided. Also, the main reason that President Nixon vetoed the bill was that the large price tag would be inflationary. In his veto message he stated that "the pressure for full funding under this bill would be so intense that funds approaching the *maximum authorized* amount could ultimately be claimed and paid out, no matter what technical controls the bill appears to grant the executive."[95]

In urging the House to override the veto, Representative Harsha stated:

> We have known all along that it would take a massive amount of money and time to reclaim and to protect our precious water resources. But, we dare not measure the cost of this water bill merely in terms of dollars alone. The question is not, "Can we afford to spend $18 billion over the next 3 years for waste treatment plants?" but "Can we afford not to?"[96]

The states argued that since Congress had passed the bill over the president's veto it fully intended the money to be spent despite the objections of those who thought the funds were excessive.

The government, on the other hand, argued that the amendments introduced by Representative Harsha and their adoption by the conference committee demonstrated a congressional intent to grant spending discretion to the administrator. Representative Harsha is quoted explaining his amendments: "I want to point out that the elimination of the word 'all' before the word 'sums' in Sec. 205(a) and the insertion of the phrase 'not to exceed' in Sec. 207 was intended by the managers of the Bill to emphasize the President's flexibility to control the rate of spending."[97] Congressmen Ford added: "The language is not a mandatory requirement for full obligation and expenditure up to the authorization figure in each of the 3 fiscal years."[98] Senator Muskie is also quoted:

> Under the Amendments proposed by Congressman Harsha and others the authorizations for obligational authority are "not to exceed" $18 billion over the next 3 years. Also, "all" sums authorized to be obligated need not be committed, though they must be allocated. These two provisions were suggested to give the administration some flexibility concerning the obligation of construction grant funds.[99]

These statements are taken by the government to demonstrate that Congress did not intend to mandate the allotment of the full amounts authorized. In litigation, most of the district courts did not agree.[100]

It must be made clear that the issue in question in all of the district courts except the Campaign Clean Water case was whether the *allotment*, not the *obligation*, of funds was mandatory or discretionary. On the basis of the language of of Section 205(a) and the legislative history, most of the district courts agreed with Senator Muskie's statement that funds must be allotted to the states, though the EPA has discretion at the obligation stage. The EPA was ordered by the courts to allot the full amounts provided by the act. However, Judge Gignoux of the U.S. District Court in Maine directed that the funds allotted pursuant to his order not be made available for obligation pending appeal and further order of the Court. Judge Lord of Minnesota in dicta also added that even if allotment was discretionary, it would be an abuse of discretion for the administrator to "substitute his sense of national priorities for that of the Congress,"[101] as he did in this case.

In *Campaign Clean Water, Inc.* v. *Ruckelshaus*[102] Judge Merhige agreed with the plaintiffs and the government that "Congress did intend for the executive branch to exercise some discretion with respect to allotments." However, that was not the issue being litigated. The organization, Campaign Clean Water, Inc., contended that the impoundment of 55 percent of the funds provided in the Water Pollution Control Act constituted an abuse of discretion in that it contravened the intent of Congress that the federal government commit extensive resources to the control of water pollution. The Court based its opinion primarily on the syntactical history of the act and the override of the presidential veto. Judge Merhige concluded: "The Court is well satisfied that the challenged impoundment policy, by which 55 percent of the allocated funds will be withheld is a violation of the spirit, intent and letter of the Act and a flagrant abuse of executive discretion."[103] The Court, however, denied injunctive relief due to the lack of the expertise required to administer the act; only declaratory relief was granted.

The Appeals Process

The Circuit Courts of Appeal

Two of the water pollution control cases were decided by the Circuit Courts of Appeal: *New York City* v. *Train*[104] (Train replacing Ruckelshaus as administrator of EPA) and *Campaign Clean Water, Inc.* v. *Train.*[105] The issue in *New York City* was allotment and the issue in *Campaign Clean Water* was obligation. In *New York City* Judges Tamm, Robinson, and Wilkey agreed with the District Court as to the jurisdictional question of sovereign immunity, and affirmed its ruling on the merits. They concluded that discretion over allotments would constitute discretion over amounts available to be spent, and would give the executive the power to contravene the intent of Congress. The Court ruled that the only question at bar was whether Secton 205(a) mandated the allotment of the full sums authorized in Section 207. It agreed with the argument of the city and affirmed the District Court ruling.

On December 10, 1973, the Fourth Circuit Court of Appeals decided the case of *Campaign Clean Water, Inc.* v. *Train*.[106] The issue was whether the District Court erred in finding that the refusal of the EPA administrator to allot and obligate 55 percent of the water pollution control funds was an abuse of discretion. (It was conceded that some discretion existed at the allotment stage.) Judge Russell accepted the decision of the District Court that procedural barriers did not bar the suit from being heard. He also found that the question of whether or not administrative discretion had been abused was reviewable by the Court.

> When the executive exercises its responsibility under appropriation legislation in such a manner as to frustrate the Congressional purpose, either by absolute refusal to spend or by a withholding of so substantial an amount of the appropriation as to make impossible the attainment of the legislative goals, the executive trespasses beyond the range of its legal discretion and presents an issue of constitutional dimensions which is obviously open to judicial review [footnote deleted].[107]

The Court, however, remanded the case to the district court.

The district court found the allotment of only 55 percent of the funds available to be contrary to the will of Congress. Judge Russell noted, however, that the administrator averred that he fully supported the goals stated in the act, but that, due to technical and economic reasons, those goals could not be achieved by immediate allotment of the funds. The Court concluded that the District Court was not necessarily incorrect, but that it made its conclusions based on insufficient evidence. The case was remanded with instructions for the District Court to examine whether or not the standards used by the administrator in fixing the allotment were "relevant" to a proper construction of the Act. Although the opinion supported the government's claim in the New York City case, it rejected the major claim that the matter was within the administrator's discretion and thus not subject to judicial review.

On April 29, 1974, the Supreme Court granted certiorari to the consolidated cases of New York City and Campaign Clean Water, Inc.

The Supreme Court

Oral argument in the Train cases was heard on November 12, 1974. Solicitor General Bork argued the case for the government and, in keeping with the government's brief, tried to construe the issue as narrowly as possible. He claimed there was no constitutional question presented but merely a matter of statutory construction. He also disclosed for the first time that the government intended to spend the full amount provided in the act, only the timing was at issue. This intention by the government had not been disclosed in previous litigation or in its brief. Chief Justice Burger indicated in a question to counsel W. Thomas Jacks that this seemed to undercut the argument of Campaign Clean Water, Inc. It did not, however, affect the argument of New York City that the funds had to be allotted, rather than actually obligated.

The cases were decided on February 18, 1975, with no dissents and Mr. Justice Douglas concurring, but writing no opinion, in each case. Mr. Justice White wrote the opinion of the Court in *Train* v. *New York City* and rested the holding on narrow grounds. The lower court decisions were affirmed and it was held that the Environmental Protection Agency must allot the funds provided in the Water Pollution Control Act Amendments. "As we view the legislative history, the indications are that the power to control, such as it was, was to be exercised at the point where funds were obligated and not in connection with the threshold function of allotting funds to the States.[108] Such a holding, narrowly construed, does not have broad implications for the rest of the impoundment litigation.

This does not necessarily mean, however, that the effect of the decision will be as narrow as the holding. In what must be considered obiter dicta, considering the actual holding, the Court said:

> As conceived and passed in both Houses, the legislation was intended to provide a firm commitment of substantial sums within a relatively limited period of time in an effort to achieve an early solution of what was deemed an urgent problem. We cannot believe that Congress at the last minute scuttled the entire effort by providing the Executive with the seemingly limitless power to withhold funds from allotment and obligation.[109]

This is a rather strong statement about congressional intent and shows a willingness of the Court to make inferences about the nature of spending measures. The decision also puts to rest previous claims by the government that the president has the inherent power to impound congressionally appropriated funds. If he had such powers, a statute such as the one in question could not take it away.

In *Train* v. *Campaign Clean Water* the Court in a per curiam opinion vacated the Court of Appeals decision. The reasoning of the Court was that in *New York City* they had found no discretion at the allotment stage, whereas the Circuit Court in *Campaign Clean Water, Inc.*, admitted some discretion at that stage. Because of this discrepancy the case was remanded.[110] By this device the Court refused to consider the merits of Campaign Clean Water's case, which had argued that a 55 percent cut in funds exceeded the discretion of the administrator. Given the dicta of the Court in *New York City* (above) it would seem that the Court might agree with *Campaign Clean Water* on the merits but did not want to decide the case. If the Court had wanted to make a decision, it does not seem that a minor concession to the government in Campaign Clean Water's argument would have prevented it from doing so.

The Impoundment litigation has shown the federal judiciary willing to adjudicate claims brought by a variety of parties challenging actions, or inactions, by the executive branch. The cases are based on the underlying assumption that Congress has the power of the purse and that the president was illegally impinging upon that power. Holdings in specific cases were usually limited to the language of appropriations statutes, and the Supreme Court decisions have been narrow statutory constructions. The effect of the litigation, however, has been a general rebuff to the claims of the executive branch that the president possesses broad authority to impound funds.

Notes

1. Edward S. Corwin, *The President* (New York: New York University Press, 1957), p. 9.
2. 1 Cranch 137 (1803).
3. 297 U.S. 288 (1936).
4. Corwin, *The President,* p. 17.
5. 4 Wallace 475 (1867), quoted in C. Herman Pritchett, *The American Constitution* (New York: McGraw-Hill, 1959), p. 150.
6. 272 U.S. 52 (1926).
7. The president's power of appointment was subsequently modified in Humphrey's Executor v. U.S., 295 U.S. 602 (1935).
8. 299 U.S. 304 (1936).
9. 369 U.S. 186 (1962).
10. Youngstown Sheet and Tube Co. v. Sawyer, 343 U.S. 579 (1952).
11. 369 US. 186 (1962).
12. Art. I, Sec. 5
13. 395 U.S. 486 (1969).
14. Ibid.
15. 92 S.Ct. 2125 (1972).
16. 403 U.S. 713 (1971).
17. U.S. v. Nixon, 94 S.Ct. 3090 (1974).
18. Ibid.
19. Youngstown Sheet and Tube Co. v. Sawyer, 343 U.S. 579, 597 (1952), concurring.
20. *The Bill of Rights* (Cambridge, Mass.: Harvard University Press, 1959), pp. 6-16.
21. Robert H. Jackson, *The Struggle for Judicial Supremacy* (New York: Vintage, 1941), p. 9.
22. 94 S.Ct. 3090 (1974).
23. San Francisco Redevelopment Agency v. Nixon, 329 F. Supp. 672 (N.D. Cal. 1971).

24. See J. D. Williams, "The Impounding of Funds by the Bureau of the Budget," *The Inter-University Case Program* no. 28, (1955), in U.S., Congress, Senate, Committee on the Judiciary, Subcommittee on Separation of Powers, *Executive Impoundment of Appropriated Funds*, 92nd Cong., 1st sess., 1971, p. 378, passim.

25. Ibid.

26. See the amicus curiae brief for the consolidated water pollution control cases submitted by the Center for Governmental Responsibility, Holland Law Center, University of Florida, Gainesville, Florida, case nos. 73-1377 and 73-1378 (1973), p. 45.

27. Quoted in Andrew J. Glass, "Congress weighs normal procedures to overturn Nixon impoundment policy," *National Journal* 5, no. 7 (17 February 1973):236.

28. See Chapter 3, for President Nixon's departure from precedent.

29. Jon Mills and Harold Levinson, "Abbreviated Findings of the Executive Impoundment Project," (Gainesville, Florida: Holland Law Center, University of Florida), p. 20.

30. For partisan political uses of impoundment, see Norman Pine, "The Impoundment Dilemma: Crisis in Constitutional Goverment," *Yale Review of Law and Social Action* 3, no. 2 (Winter 1973):99.

31. 88 Stat. 297, Public Law 93-344, 93d Congress, passed July 12, 1974.

32. John R. Schmidhauser and Larry L. Berg, *The Supreme Court and Congress* (New York: The Free Press, 1972), p. 3.

33. Rooney v. Lynn, C.A. no. 2010-73, filed July 30, 1974.

34. 86 Stat. 816, 33 U.S.C. ch. 26, Sec. 1251 et seq, Public Law 92-500.

35. *Congressional Quarterly Weekly Report* 30, no. 43 (21 October 1972):2769.

36. Ibid.

37. U.S., Congress, Senate, *Congressional Record*, October 17, 1972 (daily ed.), p. S18534.

38. City of New York v. Ruckelshaus, Brief for the Plaintiff, in U.S., Congress, Senate, Ad Hoc Subcommittee on Impoundment of Funds of the Committee on Government Operations and the Subcommittee on Separation of Powers of the Committee of the Judiciary, *Impoundment of Appropriated Funds by the President*, Joint Hearings on S. 373, 93d Cong., 1st sess., 1973, p. 945.

39. Art. I, Sec. 8.

40. Art. III, Sec. 2.

41. 28 U.S.C. Sec. 1361 (1970).

42. Stuart Glass, analyst, *Presidential Impoundment of Congressionally Appropriated Funds: An Analysis of Recent Federal Court Decisions,* U.S., Library of Congress, Congressional Research Service, 25 March 1974, no. 74-82A, p. 68.

43. 28 U.S.C. 1331 (1970).

44. Baker v. Carr, 369 U.S. 186, 204 (1962).

45. Flast v. Cohen, 392 U.S. 83, 102 (1968).

46. 5 E.R.C. 1803 (C.D. Cal., Sept. 7, 1973), no. 73-154-AAH, no. 73-736-AAH.

47. Glass, "Presidential Impoundment," p. 47.

48. C.A. no. 371-73, 358 F. Supp. 60 (D.D.C. 1973).

49. 5 E.R.C. 1586 (D.C. Minn. 26 June 1973) no. 4-73 Civ. 133.

50. Ibid.

51. 361 F. Supp. 689 (1973).

52. Ibid., p. 693.

53. No. 72 C 3044, (U.S.D.C. N.D. III. June 29, 1973).

54. 5 E.R.C. 1803 (C.D. Cal., Sept. 7, 1973).

55. Rooney v. Lynn, C.A. no. 2010-73 (D.D.C. 1974).

56. Housing and Urban Development Act of 1965, 42 U.S.C. Sec. 1302(a), Sec. 702 (1965).

57. U.S., Congress, House, *Congressional Record,* "Conclusions of Law," 2 August 1974 (daily ed.), p. H7595.

58. See, e.g., Commonwealth of Pennsylvania v. Lynn, C.A. no. 990-73 (D.D.C., 23 July 1973); Berends v. Butz, 357 F. Supp., 143 (D. Minn. 1973); Louisiana v. Weinberger, C.A. no. 73-1763 (E.D. La., 30 Nov. 1973).

59. Snyder v. Harris, 394 U.S. 332 (1969); Zahn v. International Paper Co., 414 U.S. 291 (1973).

60. Eisen v. Carlisle & Jacquelin et al., C.A. no. 73-203 (1974), Supreme Court Slip Opinion, p. 15.

61. Ibid., p. 20.

62. The doctrine goes back to Chisolm v. Georgia, 2 Dall. 419 (1973).

63. U.S., *Statutes at Large,* vol. 28, U.S.C. Sec. 1491 (1970).

64. Land v. Dollar, 330 U.S. 731, 738 (1947).

65. Dugan v. Rank, 372 U.S. 609, 620 (1963).

66. San Francisco Redevelopment Agency v. Nixon, 329 F. Supp. 672 (N.D. Cal. 1971); and Housing Authority of City and County of San Francisco v. HUD, 340 F. Supp. 654 (N.D. Cal. 1972).

67. 372 U.S. 609 (1963).

68. 361 F. Supp. 689 (E.D.Va. 1973), pp. 694-95.

69. 209 U.S. 123 (1908).

70. 5 U.S.C. Sec. 702 (1970).

71. See Brief for the Government in the consolidated water pollution control cases (1973 nos. 73-1377 and 73-1378), pp. 38-39.

72. 479 F.2d 1099 (8th Cir. 1973).

73. 358 F. Supp. 60 (D.D.C. 1973).

74. See, e.g., Campaign Clean Water, Inc. v. Ruckelshaus, 361 F. Supp. 689, 695 (E.D.Va. 1973).

75. U.S., Congress, House, *Congressional Record*, 29 March 1972 (daily ed.), p. H2727.

76. But cf. Brief for the Government in the consolidated water pollution control cases (1973 nos. 73-1377 and 73-1378), pp. 25-27.

77. Minnesota v. Fri, 5 E.R.C. 1586 (D.C. Minn. 26 June 1973) no. 4-73 Civ. 133.

78. 369 U.S. 186, 217 (1962).

79. *Impeachment: The Constitutional Problem* (Cambridge: Harvard University Press, 1973), p. 108.

80. 329 F. Supp., 672 (N.D.Cal. 1971).

81. 362 F. Supp. 1363 (D.D.C. 23 July 1973).

82. City of New York v. Ruckelshaus, 358 F. Supp. 669 (1973), p. 675.

83. Campaign Clean Water, Inc. v. Ruckelshaus, 361 F. Supp. 689 (E. D. Va. 1973), p. 696.

84. Ibid.

85. See Glass, *Presidential Impoundment,* p. 15.

86. 23 U.S.C. Sec. 101 et seq. (1970).

87. 86 Stat. 816 (1972).

88. 479 F.2d 1099 (8th Cir. 1973).

89. Brief for the respondent, Train v. Campaign Clean Water, Inc., 73-1378 (1973).

90. See e.g., Berends v. Butz, 357 F. Supp. 143 (D. Minn. 1973); Local 2677 A.F.G.E. v. Phillips, 358 F. Supp. 60 (D.D.C. 1973); Commonwealth of Pennsylvania v. Lynn, 362 F. Supp. 1363 (D.D.C. 23 July 1973).

91. 86 Stat. 816 (1972).

92. Ibid.

93. Ibid.

94. 358 F. Supp. 669 (1973), p. 677.

95. U.S., Congress, House, *Congressional Record,* 18 October 1972 (daily ed.), p. H10266.

96. Ibid., pp. H10268-69.

97. U.S., Congress, House, *Congressional Record,* 118, p. H9122.

98. Ibid., p. H9123.

99. Ibid., p. S16871.

100. See, e.g., City of New York v. Ruckelshaus, 358 F. Supp. 669 (1973); Minnesota v. Fri, 5 E.R.C. 1586 (D.C. Minn. 26 June 1973) no. 4-73 Civ. 133; Martin-Tricona v. Ruckelshaus, no. 72-C3044 (N.D. Ill. 29 June 1973); Texas v. Ruckelshaus, C.A. no. A-73-CA-38 (W.D. Tex. 1973); Florida v. Train, Civ. no. 73-156 (N.D. Fla., 1974); Maine v. Train, Civ. no. 14-51 (D. Maine, 1974); Ohio v. E.P.A., nos. C. 73-1061 and C. 74-104 (N.D. Ohio, 1974).

101. Minnesota v. Fri, no. 4-73 Civ. 133 (D. Minn., 26 June 1973).

102. 362 F. Supp. 689 (E. D. Va. 1973).

103. Ibid., p. 700.

104. 6 E.R.C. 1177 (23 January 1974).

105. 489 F.2d 492 (10 December 1973).

106. Ibid.

107. Ibid., p. 498.

108. Slip Opinion, p. 11. 420 U.S. 35, p. 48.

109. Slip Opinion, pp. 8-10. 420 U.S. 35, pp. 45-46.

110. See Slip Opinion, p. 2. 420 U.S. 136.

6
The Political Context
of Budget Reform

The early 1940s marked the beginning of congressional opposition to presidential impoundment of funds, though reaction was sporadic and clouded by the war. The Legislative Reorganization Act of 1946 contained a potentially major budget reform but the will to implement it was absent. The Omnibus Appropriations Act of 1950 was an attempt at budgetary comprehensiveness, but it also foundered. In the 1950s and 1960s attempts at budget reform focussed primarily on the executive branch and managerial effectiveness, the foremost example being the experiment with Planning Programming Budgeting Systems. The first part of this chapter will examine the budget reform attempt of 1946. The reasons for its failure were instructive to the framers of the 1974 reform.

A theme throughout this study has been that relations between the president and Congress during the Nixon administration were particularly strained. This situation existed in other issue areas as well as in conflicts over the budgetary power. The latter part of this chapter examines congressional reactions to presidential power in the use of the pocket veto, the attempted dismantling of the Office of Economic Opportunity, and the War Powers Resolution. Finally, conflicts in the budgetary arena will be dealt with, particularly the establishment of the joint study committee that directly led to the Congressional Budget and Impoundment Control Act of 1974.

Previous Budget Reform Attempts

The Legislative Budget of 1946

The growth in the size and power of the federal government during World War II led to consideration of proposals for congressional reform. A Joint Committee on the Organization of Congress was set up in February 1945 to study various proposals. The resulting Legislative Reorganization Act of 1946 (**P.L.** 79-601) instituted large-scale changes in the internal procedures of Congress. Most notably the committee structure was streamlined, the number of standing committees reduced in the House from forty-eight to nineteen and in the Senate from thirty-three to fifteen. Legislators' salaries were increased and staff services were improved. In an attempt to let Congress deal more comprehensively with the budget and assert congressional budget priorities more effectively, the act provided for a legislative budget.[1]

Section 138 set up a Joint Committee on the Budget consisting of the members of the House Ways and Means and Appropriations Committees and members of the Senate Finance and Appropriations Committees. The joint committee was to consider the president's budget and recommend to the Congress by February 15 of each year a maximum amount to be appropriated for expenditure. It was to issue a report accompanied by a concurrent resolution adopting the ceiling on expenditures, and if expenditures exceeded estimated receipts, it was to include a section stating: "That it is the sense of the Congress that the public debt shall be increased in an amount equal to the amount by which the estimated expenditures for the ensuing fiscal year exceed the estimated receipts, such amount being $—."[2]

The purpose of Section 138 was to remedy several widely recognized deficiencies in the congressional budgetary process. There was no occasion for Congress to consider revenues and expenditures at the same time in relation to each other. The House and Senate acted separately and the House Appropriations Committee was fragmented into isolated subcommittees.[3] The legislative budget was intended to give Congress the opportunity to take an overall view of the budget and impose a spending ceiling upon itself, thus acting in a more coherent manner than before. In addition, the bill was to strengthen the Congress as opposed to the executive branch in the budgetary arena. According to the Committee on the Reorganization of Congress, "The executive has mingled appropriations, brought forward and backward unexpended and anticipated balances, incurred coercive deficiencies, and otherwise escaped the rigors of congressional control."[4] This was in part a reassertion of congressional prerogatives, but it was also in part a partisan attempt of the Republican Congress to assert its priorities over the Democratic administration. It was also expected that the legislative budget would result in a balanced budget, and it thus received widespread support in and out of Congress.[5]

The operation of the act, however, did not live up to the expectations of its framers. In 1947 a concurrent resolution passed the House calling for a $6 billion cut in the president's budget with the unspent funds to be used in retiring part of the national debt and providing a tax cut. But in the Senate an amendment was adopted that would have cut the president's expenditure estimate only $4.5 billion. The bill became deadlocked in conference and no legislative budget was adopted for fiscal 1948. The impasse was due to disagreement over the size of the cut in the budget and the disposal of the surplus.[6]

In 1948 both houses agreed on the same legislative budget that called for a $2.5 billion cut in the executive budget, but the form these cuts would take was not specified. The resolution seemed to have no teeth and Congress appropriated $6 billion more than the proposed cuts.[7] In 1949 the deadline for the concurrent resolution was moved back from February 15 to May 1 and by that time most appropriations had already passed the House and Senate with the result that no legislative budget was produced that year. In 1950 there was not even an attempt to formulate a legislative budget.

One of the main reasons for the failure to implement the legislative budget successfully is that it was perceived as a political tool to be used against the opposition party. The Joint Committee on the Reorganization of Congress stated: "Congress has long lacked adequate facilities for the continuous inspection and review of administrative agencies within their jurisdiction."[8] Representative Clarence Cannon argued that the Republican party "attempted to use the legislative budget as a stepping stone in pursuit of its tax program."[9] Jesse Burkhead also considers partisan factors to have played a part in the failure. "Certainly the whole Reorganization Act is shot through with a punitive philosophy of putting the administration in its place."[10]

One does not have to rely on partisan differences, however, to explain the failure of the legislative budget. One of the main drawbacks of the legislation was the February 15 deadline for the spending ceiling. This did not give the committee adequate time for study of the budget and forced it to make decisions before considering the various components in detail.[11] Also there was no provision for amendment of the ceiling, thereby creating a rigid structure that could not change with new circumstances but had to stand or fall in its original formulation.[12] Congress was not willing to bind itself to a hard ceiling six months before the beginning of the fiscal year.[13] Clarence Cannon said: "we can no more expect success . . . with this well-meant but hopeless proposal than we can expect a verdict from the jury before it has heard the evidence."[14] Ironically this rigidity resulted in a ceiling with no teeth that could be ignored by the appropriations committees, as happened in 1948.[15] The dilemma of rigidity versus complete lack of enforcement provisions was a major concern of the framers of the 1974 Budget Act.

Another problem in the attempted implementation of the legislative budget was the failure of the joint committee to specify where the large cuts were to come out of the budget. The Republicans wanted the credit for budget cutting without the onus of specifying whose funds were to be cut. The minority members of the joint committee stated: "No itemized estimate of major reductions has been submitted either in the majority report or in the discussion of the resolution proposed by the report. As a matter of fact, no information is available upon which to predicate such an estimate."[16] In addition to the above political and practical problems, the joint committee was so large as to be unwieldy, with a total of 102 members. In addition, the committee had no permanent staff of its own, thus having to rely largely on other congressional staff and information supplied by the Budget Bureau.[17] The Budget Act of 1974 was formulated with the 1940s experience in mind and was to attempt to overcome many of the difficulties inherent in Section 138 of the Reorganization Act of 1946.

The Omnibus Appropriations Bill

With the failure of the legislative budget Congress decided to make another attempt to introduce a greater degree of coherence into the budgetary process. In hearings over the proposed Legislative Reorganization Act of 1946, Budget Director Harold Smith testified that "a more consistent Congressional policy could probably be achieved in appropriations by consolidating all annual appropriation bills into a single measure."[18] That proposal was not incorporated into the 1946 act but in 1947 it was incorporated into a Senate concurrent resolution sponsored by Senators Harry F. Byrd of Virginia and Butler of Nebraska.[19] No action was taken by the Senate at that time but a similar measure passed the Senate in September 1949. Although the House did not act on the resolution, Representative Cannon announced that the House Appropriations Committee would adopt an omnibus appropriations system in the next session of Congress.[20] He considered it an internal committee procedure and thus not dependent upon a concurrent resolution.

In spring of 1950 the Congress considered the appropriations for fiscal 1951 with Senate and House Appropriations subcommittees holding hearings during the same period to facilitate consideration of the omnibus bill. The procedures within the appropriations committees were not greatly different from previous years.[21] The Omnibus Appropriations Bill (H.R. 7786) was approved by the House on May 10, 1950, but was not passed by the Senate until August 28. President Truman signed the bill on September 6, 1950. This was two months before the budget was completed in 1949 and more than

$2 billion was cut from the president's budget.[22] This was not the full picture, however. In fiscal 1951 a total of five deficiency and supplemental appropriations acts had to be passed. While part of these were due to the unexpected Korean War, the purpose of the single appropriations bill was not fulfilled.[23]

The conclusion of Chairman Cannon after the 1950 experience with the omnibus appropriations process was that "the single appropriations bill offers the most practical and efficient method of handling the annual budget and the national fiscal program."[24] Despite Cannon's enthusiasm the House Appropriations Committee met in January 1951 and voted thirty-one to eighteen to abandon the new practice.[25] The Senate Appropriations Committee also opposed the omnibus system.[26]

Representative Cannon's position was that "Every predatory lobbyist, every pressure group seeking to get its hands into the United States Treasury, every bureaucrat seeking to extend his empire downtown" was opposed to the omnibus system.[27] The issue, however, cannot be that clearly delineated. Representative Phillips has argued that a one-package budget is extremely vulnerable to pork barrel, despite the fact that in the 1950 act, pork barrel was minimized. He claimed that it is easy to hide individual spending items within large appropriations bills where they will be overlooked because of the necessity to examine the larger items.[28] This is consistent with criticisms that the omnibus appropriation was too massive for individual members to give it careful consideration.[29] From a different perspective it is argued that an omnibus bill is more open to "meat axe" (across the board cuts in spending), a particularly nondiscriminating means of spending reduction.[30]

An additional objection to the consolidated appropriations bill is that even more power is concentrated in the hands of the Appropriations Committees.[31] Saloma has argued that this intensification of the traditional disparity in power between the appropriations and legislative committees may have contributed to the bill's defeat in 1951.[32] In 1953 the Senate again voted to adopt an omnibus system but the House refused to act on the proposal, and it has not been adopted since.

President Nixon and the Congress

The Breakdown of Comity

In his book, *The Imperial Presidency*, Arthur Schlesinger argues that the Nixon presidency was marked by a breakdown of comity between the president and Congress. The concept of comity is vague, but it is meant to connote a degree of restraint in interbranch relations that allows informal norms to keep disputes from getting out of hand. This section will briefly examine three instances in which the perceived breakdown of comity by the Congress led it to react, sometimes through the courts, to limit presidential actions. The special use of the pocket veto and the attempted dismantling of the Office of Economic Opportunity were clearly unique to the Nixon presidency. The War Powers Resolution was a reaction to broader historical trends, but it is significant that it was passed during President Nixon's tenure in office.

The Pocket veto. One of the disputes between President Nixon and Congress involved the use of the pocket veto. The Constitution provides that when the Congress sends a bill to the president: "If any Bill shall not be returned by the President within ten Days (Sundays excepted) after it shall have been presented to him, the Same shall be a Law, in like manner as if he had signed it, unless the Congress by their Adjournment prevent its Return, in which Case it shall not be a Law."[33] This procedure is called a pocket veto and has generally occurred at the final adjournment of Congress or at the end of a session.

Before the 1940s Congress seldom adjourned within a session, and so pocket vetoes during a session were rare.[34] Before President Nixon there were only sixty-four pocket vetoes that occurred during a session of Congress. Most of these were private bills and the adjournments during which they occurred were usually of one month or longer.

On December 14, 1970, Congress sent to President Nixon S. 3418, the Family Practice of Medicine Act, which authorized $225 million for hospitals and medical schools for the establishment of special programs in family medicine and paramedical training. On December 22 Congress adjourned for a five-day Christmas holiday, though the Senate authorized the secretary of the senate to receive messages from the president. On December 24, 1970, President Nixon issued a Memorandum of Disapproval announcing that S. 3418 was pocket vetoed.

There was a feeling in Congress that President Nixon was abusing the pocket veto by asserting it during a five-day recess. It was felt, since the bill had passed the House by 346-2 and the Senate by 64-1, that he was trying to avoid an almost certain override if he had sent Congress a veto message.

Senator Edward Kennedy went to court to challenge this unprecedented use of the pocket veto. Judge Joseph Waddy heard the case and issued his decision on August 15, 1973.[35] In his opinion he emphasized that a bill would become law "unless the Congress by their Adjournment *prevent* its Return" (emphasis added) and that the Senate had provided for the receiving of messages from the president. Although this was not a major incident, it illustrates what Congress perceived to be a breach of comity, or traditional norms.

The dismantling of OEO. When President Nixon submitted his budget for 1974 it did not include any funds for continuation of the Office of Economic Opportunity (OEO), which had been administering President Johnson's War on Poverty. He had also appointed Howard J. Phillips to be acting director of the agency. Phillips began to dismantle OEO and phase out its programs by administrative direction and the withholding of funds. The rationale for the action was that OEO activities were not within the priorities of the administration, and it had requested no funds for their continuation.

The response from the Congress was negative. In the first place many members of the Democratic majority were the same members who had passed the original legislation and disagreed with the president's evaluation of OEO's usefulness. Secondly, the Economic Opportunity Act was extended in September 1972 and funds had been appropriated through June 30, 1973. It apeared that the president's budget proposals were being forced and that the Economic Opportunity Act was being disregarded. Senator Nelson said that the dismantling of OEO reflected a lack of respect for existing law and for the Congress. . . . To do so in direct defiance of specific legislation passed by the Congress and signed by the President, is most surprising behavior in an Administration that recommends obedience to the law as the citizen's first duty.[36]

Suit was brought in court by Local 2677 of the American Federation of Government Employees claiming that the dismantling of OEO constituted actions contrary to the legislation setting up the agency.[37] Judge William B. Jones heard the case and ruled that the discontinuance of a program in the face of multiple year authorizations and appropriations until the end of the fiscal year were unlawful and beyond the statutory authority of the acting director, Phillips. He concluded that "historical precedent, logic, and the text of the Constitution itself obligate the defendant to continue to operate the . . . programs as was intended by the Congress, and not terminate them."[38] He also ruled that past actions of Phillips to dismantle the agency were null and void.

In another case the appointment of Howard Phillips as acting director of OEO was challenged because his name had not been submitted to the Senate for confirmation.[39] Senator Harrison A. Williams charged that President Nixon was trying to get around the Senate's duty to advise and consent by treating Phillips as an acting director and then not submitting his name. "The combination of these two actions—the deliberate abuse of senatorial prerogatives, and the cavalier destruction of so many worthwhile social and economic programs, clearly could not go unheeded."[40] The court ruled for the plaintiff and held that in the absence of special legislation providing for an acting director "the constitutional process of nomination and confirmation must be followed." It concluded that Phillips was holding his job unlawfully and enjoined him from taking any actions as director of OEO.[41]

The War Powers Resolution. One of the major sources of conflict between the president and Congress since President Nixon took office was the war in Indochina. Many members of Congress were growing increasingly disenchanted with the war, and from 1969 to 1973 there had been more than ninety votes on antiwar measures in Congress.[42] In 1969 and 1970 Congress voted to stop funds for U.S. ground combat forces in Laos, Thailand, and Cambodia. Also in 1971 an amendment was added to the Defense Procurement Authorization Act stating that it was "the policy of the United States to terminate at the earliest practicable date all military operations of the United States in Indochina." President Nixon signed the bill but said that the declaration did "not represent the policies of the Administration," and that it was "without binding force or effect."[43]

In spring of 1973 the movement in Congress to end U.S. involvement in Indochina did not slow with the withdrawal of U.S. ground combat troops. In May an amendment by Senator Thomas Eagleton to cut off funds for any combat activity in or over Cambodia or Laos was attached to a supplemental appropriations bill.[44] When President Nixon vetoed the bill Senator Mike Mansfield threatened to attach the same amendment to future bills and it was attached to several other measures. With a showdown approaching, Congress and the president reached a compromise on June 29 that postponed the funds' cutoff until August 15.

The most important challenge to the president's ability to wage war, however, came in the War Powers Resolution. The major provisions of the resolution provided that if the president introduced troops into a foreign nation he would have to withdraw them within sixty days unless Congress had declared war or extended the period. The president would extend the period for thirty days if he verified that it was necessary for the safe withdrawal of the forces. However, the Congress could pass a concurrent resolution at any time directing the president to withdraw the forces.

Proponents of the resolution saw it as "the historic opportunity to reassert [the Congress'] constitutionally mandated obligation in the area of war powers."[45] Conservative opponents thought it would hamper the president in a crisis situation. Ironically, liberal opponents saw the resolution as granting the president more power than he had under the Constitution. Senator Eagleton saw the resolution as dangerous because it gave the president "an open, blank check" to "take us to war. It is a horrible mistake."[46]

President Nixon opposed the resolution because "the restrictions which this resolution would impose upon the authority of the President are both unconstitutional and dangerous to the best interests of our Nation."[47] He felt that it was an attempt to take away constitutional war powers through legislation and an attempt to get around the veto provision by mandating the withdrawal of forces pursuant to a concurrent resolution. In a message to the House of Representatives he said, "The only way in which the constitutional powers of a branch of the Government can be altered is by amending the Constitution—and any attempt to make such alterations by legislation alone is clearly without force."[48] The War Powers Resolution was finally passed over President Nixon's veto by votes of 284-135 in the House and 75-18 in the Senate.

The Budgetary Arena

In addition to the normal friction between the president and Congress over the budget (such as shifting the blame for deficits and partisan differences), the past several decades have seen congressional attempts to redress the institutional balance. With the Nixon presidency, however, these clashes took on the air of a constitutional crisis. A breakdown of comity took place in many areas and particularly with regard to budget control. Such was the state of affairs when Congress formulated the 1974 Budget Act.

It is difficult to assess the impact of the Watergate-related events and subsequent impeachment proceedings on this series of congressional/presidential interactions. The assertion of executive privilege certainly added to the air of confrontation between the two branches. One point of view argues that at the time the impact of Watergate was to weaken the political position of the presidency enough to make congressional legislation limiting presidential power easier to pass.

The counter hypothesis is that, Watergate aside, the interaction between President Nixon and the Congress was so hostile that other points of disagreement would have been even more augmented. That is, if Watergate had not happened, impoundment would have been a much more salient point of contention. However, it can be argued that despite such speculation, the substance of the struggle over budgetary power was important enough that the outcome in terms of legislative and judicial actions would not have been significantly different in the absence of Watergate.

While the conflict between President Nixon and the Congress discussed above provides a context, an account of the breakdown of comity over fiscal priorities and budgetary power is the focus of this study. The impoundment aspects of this clash have been discussed in previous chapters; other budgetary interactions are the present concern. Arguing over fiscal policy is a traditional game played by the two branches, with each claiming that it is responsible for saving more money than the other. Presidential advisor John Ehrlichman spoke about the "credit-card Congress" that was recklessly spending money without regard for the revenue necessary to cover outlays.[49]

President Nixon tied his accusations of congressional fiscal irresponsibility to "the hoary and traditional procedure of the Congress which now permits action on the various spending programs as if they were unrelated and independent actions."[50] The congressional reaction was to continue to pursue its own fiscal priorities while at the same time recognizing that its own budgetary process had many deficiencies. Legislation was introduced to curb the president's control of budgetary priorities by limiting impoundment and requiring the confirmation of the OMB director by the Senate. A crucial turning point came in the fall of 1972 when the Senate refused to give the president the discretion over fiscal 1973 spending that he had asked for. A joint study committee was established that was to propose legislation that would eventually become the 1974 Budget Act.

Budget control bills. In the latter part of the 1960s there were many proposed bills aimed at improving control over the budget. These bills ranged from proposals granting the president an item veto on appropriations bills to proposals splitting the fiscal year into separate fiscal and legislative sessions for Congress. In the eighty-ninth Congress alone (1965-67) there were fifteen separate bills to create a Joint

Committee on the Budget.[51] None of the bills resulted in major budgetary reform, though many of the ideas contained in them were longstanding proposals for budget improvement and were incorporated in the 1974 Budget Act.

As has been explained elsewhere, President Johnson impounded substantial amounts of funds in the domestic area without creating a constitutional crisis. With the quantitative and qualitative changes in impoundment practice made by President Nixon, however, the issue became a bone of contention between the president and Congress. In the ninety-second Congress (1971-73) for the first time there were six bills introduced to require the president to notify Congress when he impounds funds.[52] In the ninety-third Congress there were at least eighteen bills introduced to limit presidential impoundment in some way.[53]

Of these bills the two that survived and became representative of the positions of the two houses were S. 373, passed May 10, 1973;[54] and H.R. 8480, passed July 25, 1973. The Senate bill provided that the president could impound funds only if Congress gave its explicit approval. The House bill would have allowed the president to impound funds unless Congress specifically ruled otherwise. The differences reflect the traditional differing perspectives of the two houses on money matters, the House being fiscally more conservative than the Senate. Congress was not able to agree on one antiimpoundment bill until the 1974 Budget Act was passed.

Confirmation of OMB director. In recognition of the powerful role of the Office of Management and Budget (OMB) and in an attempt to obtain more congressional input in budgetary policymaking, in May 1973 Congress passed S. 518, a bill requiring Senate confirmation of the director and deputy director of OMB. The bill would have applied to the incumbents, Roy Ash and Fred Malek.

On May 18, 1973, President Nixon vetoed the bill because he thought it would be "a grave violation of the fundamental doctrine of separation of powers."[55] He thought it would be unconstitutional because it would have the effect of circumventing the presidential removal power in its application to the present incumbents. He also said the advisory and staff nature of the positions required that they be controlled by the president and not subject to Senate confirmation.

The Senate overrode the veto on June 25 but the House sustained it. As a result the bill was modified to exempt the incumbents of the positions from its requirements.[56] In an attempt to avoid another veto the House also deleted a provision transferring the OMB powers from the president to the OMB director. Final action was taken by the Senate on February 6, 1974, and was signed by President Nixon on March 2.

The Joint Study Committee. In addition to the longer range pressures building a consensus in Congress on the need for budgetary reform, the immediate precipitant for the 1974 budget reform was a dispute over a spending ceiling proposal in the fall of 1972. In a message to Congress in July 1972 President Nixon argued that the current budget crisis was caused by the fiscal irresponsibility of Congress and asked for authority to hold fiscal 1973 spending to $250 billion.[57] On October 4, 1972, the House passed H.R. 16810, which would have given the president that authority while raising the debt ceiling $15 billion to a total of $465 billion. The bill would have allowed the president to cut spending as he saw fit in order to preserve the spending ceiling of $250 billion, an unprecedented granting of spending discretion.[58] Previous spending limits in fiscal 1969, 1970, and 1971 had provisions to automatically raise the ceiling as appropriations or uncontrollable spending increased.[59]

The debate in Congress over the grant of spending power to the president centered around the question of constitutional responsibility for the power of the purse. House Speaker Carl Albert opposed the provision as too broad a grant of authority. "The question before us is whether we will knowingly and willingly abdicate not only our powers, but (also) our responsibilities to the executive branch of government."[60] The administration was arguing, however, that Congress was refusing to discipline itself and was without an institutional mechanism to do so.[61] Many members of Congress who favored the House version of H.R. 16810 thought that the drastic measure of the bill was necessary. Wilber Mills was among them. "If we abdicate here any willingness to join in controlling spending . . . all . . . the President has to do is to go before the American people on television and ask for a Congress . . . that will cooperate with him in getting control of spending."[62] Many other members of Congress, particularly in the House, agreed with Mills. Richard Fenno found that in the 1972 campaign incumbents were critical of the congressional budgetary process. "Members run for Congress by running against Congress."

> One-half the Representatives I was with blasted the House for being so spineless that it gave away its power of the purse to the President. The other half blasted the House for being so spineless in exercising its power of the purse that the President had been forced to act.[63]

There was considerable concern over the likely impact this would have in the fall elections, whether the blame for increasing deficit spending would be placed on the president or Congress. The Senate, however, was not willing to give President Nixon as much authority as he had requested. The Finance Committee reported the bill out favorably, but amendments from the floor changed the act so as to limit the requested authority. Several categories of expenditures were excluded entirely from any cuts.[64]

In conference the Senate restrictions on the nature of spending cuts were diluted but still gave the president significant discretion. He could cut appropriations in fifty functional categories up to twenty percent. The Senate, however, would still not go along and rejected the conference report. Finally on October 18 a second conference report was filed and H.R. 16810 was passed without any spending ceiling or spending reduction authority given to the president.

The clash between the president and Congress over spending authority in the fall of 1972 made weaknesses in congressional budget procedures visible and salient to the legislators. The main drawback was the lack of any mechanism by which the Congress could consider the budget as a whole and choose among competing priorities. Appropriations were considered in fourteen separate bills that were not necessarily correlated with each other or with revenue. This had been a long-standing criticism of Congress, but the partisan political consequences of it became particularly evident in the fall of 1972.

The fact that Congress many times cut the president's proposed budget was nullified by backdoor spending provisions that brought spending totals up in amounts comparable to the cuts.[65] The presidential practice of impoundment was also becoming a focus of congressional discontent with its budget process. As a consequence, H.R. 16810 retained in its final form (P.L. 92-599) a provision setting up a temporary Joint Study Committee on Budget Control to reexamine the whole budgetary process and recommend to the Congress:

> the procedures which should be adopted by the Congress for the purpose of improving Congressional control of budgetary outlay and receipt totals, including procedures for establishing and maintaining an overall view of each year's budgetary outlays which is fully coordinated with an overall view of the anticipated revenues for that year.[66]

The Joint Study Committee on Budget Control, which was set up by passage of H.R. 16810, began its work of proposing budgetary changes to the Congress immediately and came out with an interim report on February 7, 1973.[67] The report, which began with a statement of goals the committee wanted to achieve, analyzed the various defects in congressional budget procedures that ought to be remedied. The final report would make more specific proposals for change.

The committee began with the assumption that Congress should have a more coherent budget process in order to make it better able to enhance its position in relation to the president and to cope with the general problems of federal revenue and spending. Mechanisms had to be developed by which Congress could consider fiscal, economic, and monetary factors in determining the proper level of federal expenditures and could enforce that limit on spending and budget authority. There also had to be a way to determine the proper levels of taxation and national debt needed to support the spending levels. These mechanisms did not exist in any effective way in the past and many budgetary problems were thus aggravated.[68]

The committee considered one of the main defects in previous congressional procedures to be the lack of an overall perspective on the budget. The House and Senate Appropriations Committees would hold hearings on the president's budget but actual decisions would be made in different places. Appropriations subcommittees reported out separate bills that did not necessarily have any relationship to each other. The priority choices represented by the separate bills were not confronted directly. Neither was there coordination between appropriations and expected revenues, for tax legislation was handled by Ways and Means in the House and Finance in the Senate. The Joint Economic Committee dealt with the president's budget and made recommendations concerning fiscal and monetary policy, but it had no direct effect on decision making through a legislative program.[69] This situation was seen by the committee to contribute substantially to the increasing national debt. From 1920 to 1974 the federal budget has been in deficit thirty-seven times and there have been only six surplusses since 1931.[70] The national debt had increased by about $200 billion in the last twenty years.[71]

Another problem with congressional handling of the budget was the loss of control by the appropriations committee of annual spending, primarily through the use of backdoor spending authority. Backdoor spending as described in Chapter 3 is budget authority that is created by substantive committees rather than the appropriations committees, and makes the control of spending more difficult. From 1969 to 1973 Congress reduced the budget requests of the president by a total of about $30 billion, yet during the same time period backdoor spending authority exceeded the budget estimates by about $30 billion.[72]

Uncontrollable expenditures have also added to the difficulty Congress has in affecting national priorities through the budget. Outlays are considered uncontrollable in one fiscal year when "government decisions in that year can neither increase nor decrease them without changing existing substantive law."[73] Relatively uncontrollable programs include social insurance trust funds, unemployment benefits, interest on the debt, and public assistance payments.[74] In order for the president or Congress to gain more control over budgetary totals there has to be a limit on future budget authority granted in any given year.

The Joint Study Committee in addition felt that any new legislation had to deal with the gap between authorizations and appropriations as well as the increasing necessity for continuing resolutions. The committee was conscious of the difficulties with the legislative budgets of the late 1940s and emphasized that spending ceilings would be a necessity in budget reform efforts. There would have to be provisions for adequate time to examine budget requests and enforcement provisions to make ceilings effective in order to avoid the pitfalls of the 1946 Act.[75]

Notes

1. See Jesse Burkhead, "Federal Budgetary Developments: 1947-1948," *Public Administration Review* 8, no. 4 (Autumn 1948):267.

2. Sec. 138(b), Legislative Reorganization Act of 1946 (P.L. 79-601).

3. See Burkhead, "Budgetary Developments," p. 267.

4. U.S., Congress, *Congressional Record,* 25 July 1946, 92, p. 10047.

5. Burkhead, "Budgetary Developments," pp. 267-68.

6. See Avery Leiserson, "Coordination of Federal Budgetary and Appropriations Procedures Under the Legislative Reorganization Act of 1946," *National Tax Journal* 1 (June 1948):118. For the former view see Clinton Fielder, "Reform of the Congressional Legislative Budget," *National Tax Journal* 4 (1951):65; and Burkhead, "Budgetary Developments," p. 268. For the latter view see *Congressional Quarterly,* "Special Report," on Congressional Reform (1 April 1964), 22, p. 32.

7. See *Congressional Quarterly,* "Special Report," p. 32.

8. U.S., Congress, *Congressional Record* 25 July 1946, 92, p. 10047.

9. Clarence Cannon, "Congressional Responsibilities," *American Political Science Review* 42 (April 1948):313.

10. Burkhead, "Budgetary Developments," p. 269. See also Louis Fisher, "Experience With a Legislative Budget (1947-1949)," in U.S.,

Congress, Senate, Subcommittee on Budgeting, Management and Expenditures, Committee on Government Operations, *Improving Congressional Control of the Budget,* Hearings, Part II, 93d Cong., 1st sess., 1973, p. 237.

11. See Fisher, "Legislative Budget," pp. 237-38.

12. See Burkhead, "Budgetary Developments," p. 269.

13. See Fielder, "Reform," p. 69.

14. U.S., Congress, *Congressional Record,* 7 February 1959, 95, pp. 879-82.

15. See Fisher, "Legislative Budget," p. 238.

16. Quoted in Cannon, "Congressional Responsibilities," p. 314.

17. See Fisher, "Legislative Budget," p. 239. For an analysis of the failure of the legislative budget see Ira Sharkansky, *The Politics of Taxing and Spending* (New York: Bobbs-Merrill, 1969), pp. 77-78. See also George B. Galloway, *The Legislative Process in Congress* (New York: Thomas Y. Crowell Co., 1955), pp. 616-20.

18. U.S., Congress, Joint Committee on the Organization of the Congress, Hearings, 79th Cong., 1st sess., 1946, p. 674.

19. John Phillips, "The Hadacol of the Budget Makers," *National Tax Journal* 4 (1951):257.

20. See Dalmas H. Nelson, "The Omnibus Appropriations Act of 1950," *Journal of Politics* 15 (1953):275. See also ibid.

21. Nelson, "The Act of 1950," pp. 278, 281.

22. Galloway, *The Legislative Process,* p. 123.

23. See Phillips, "Hadacol," p. 259.

24. Quoted in Galloway, *The Legislative Process,* p. 123.

25. Phillips, "Hadacol," p. 258.

26. See Senate Report 842, "Consolidated General Appropriation Bill," U.S., Congress, Senate, *Congressional Record,* 82d Cong., 1st sess., 1951, pp. 7-15.

27. Quoted in Galloway, *The Legislative Process,* p. 123.

28. Phillips, "Hadacol," p. 262.

29. See Nelson, "The Act of 1950," p. 278.

30. Also see Sharkansky, *The Politics,* p. 78; and John S. Saloma, "The Responsible Use of Power," in Murray L. Weidenbaum and John S. Saloma, *Congress and the Federal Budget* (Washington, D.C.: American Enterprise Institute, 1965), p. 168.

31. See Phillips, "Hadacol," pp. 260-61.

32. Saloma, "The Responsible Use of Power," pp. 166-67.

33. Art I, Sec. 7, Cl. 2.

34. See Arthur M. Schlesinger, Jr., *The Imperial Presidency* (New York: Popular Library, 1974), pp. 236-38.

35. Kennedy v. Sampson, 364 F. Supp. 1075 (1973), in U.S., Congress, Senate, *Congressional Record,* 11 September 1973 (daily ed.), p. S16297.

36. U.S., Congress, Senate, *Congressional Record,* 12 April 1973 (daily ed.), 119, p. S7333.

37. Local 2677 A.F.G.E. v. Phillips, C.A. no. 371-73, 358 F. Supp. 60 (D.D.C. 1973), ibid.

38. Ibid.

39. Williams v. Phillips, 360 F. Supp. 1363 (D.D.C. 1973).

40. U.S., Congress, Senate, *Congressional Record,* 14 June 1973 (daily ed.), p. S11151.

41. Williams v. Phillips, 360 F. Supp. 1363 (D.D.C. 1973).

42. See *Congressional Quarterly Weekly Report* 31, no. 32 (August 11, 1973):2207.

43. See Schlesinger, *The Imperial Presidency,* p. 192.

44. See *Congressional Quarterly Weekly Report* 31, no. 32 (August 11, 1973):2207.

45. See statement of Representative Zablocki, *Congressional Quarterly Weekly Report* 31, no. 45 (November 10, 1973):2986.

46. Ibid.

47. U.S., Congress, *Congressional Record,* 93d Cong., 1st sess., 7 November 1973, 119, pt.28:36175-76.

48. Ibid. There were also attempts to limit the president's war power through litigation, see e.g. Holtzman v. Schlesinger, 414 U.S. 1304 (1973).

49. For the congressional reply see Herbert Jaspar, "A Congressional Budget: Will It Work This Time," *The Bureaucrat* 3, no. 3 (January 1975):429.

50. Quoted in Louis Fisher, "The President versus Congress: Who Wins?," in Charles Roberts, ed., *Has the President Too Much Power?* (New York: Harper's Magazine Press, 1973), p. 161.

51. See Committee on Government Operations, *Improving Congressional Control,* p. 167.

52. Ibid., p. 171.

53. Ibid., pp. 173-74.

54. It was also passed as an amendment to dollar devaluation legislation on April 4, 1973, and as part of a debt ceiling bill on June 27, 1973.

55. "Presidential Veto Message," *Congressional Quarterly Weekly Report* 31, no. 21 (May 26, 1973):1293.

56. See U.S., Congress, House, *Congressional Record,* 17 December 1973 (daily ed.), p. H11544.

57. *Weekly Compilation of Presidential Documents* 8, no. 31 (26 July 1972):1176.

58. Congressional Quarterly, *1972 Almanac* (Washington D.C.: Congressional Quarterly, Inc., 1972), p. 421.

59. Ibid., p. 423.

60. Ibid., p. 420.

61. See Louis Fisher, "Congress, the Executive and the Budget," *The Annals* 411 (January 1974):102.

62. For an analysis of the attempt by President Nixon to blame the Congress for increasing deficits and inflation, see ibid.

63. Richard Fenno, "If, as Ralph Nader Says, Congress is 'The Broken Branch,' How Come We Love Our Congressmen So Much?," presented to the Harvard Club in Boston on Dec. 12, 1972, in U.S., Congress, House, *Congressional Record*, 8 March 1973, 119, pp. H1581, H1582.

64. Congressional Quarterly, *1972 Almanac*, p. 421.

65. U.S., Congress, House, Joint Study Committee on Budget Control, *Interim Report: Improving Congressional Control over Budgetary Outlay and Receipt Totals* 7 February 1973, H. Rept. 93-13, p. 8.

66. Ibid., p. 1.

67. Ibid.

68. See ibid., p. 2.

69. Ibid., p. 7.

70. See U.S., Congress, House, Joint Study Committee on Budget Control, *Recommendations for Improving Congressional Control Over Budgetary Outlay and Receipt Totals*, 18 April 1973, H. Rept. 7130, Table 1, pp. 33-34. These figures are based on the administrative budget. The unified budget—in use since 1969—would differ only by showing a surplus in 1969.

71. U.S., Congress, Senate, Senate Committee on Government Operations, *Congressional Budget Reform*, (no date), p. 3.

72. Joint Study Committee, *Improving Congressional Control*, Table 6, p. 21.

73. *The Budget of the United States Government, Fiscal Year 1976* (Washington: Government Printing Office, 1975), p. 29.

74. Joint Study Committee, *Interim Report*, p. 8.

75. Ibid., p. 11.

7
The Congressional Budget
and Impoundment Control Act
of 1974

The Joint Study Committee on Budget Control established in the fall of 1972 took its mandate seriously and came up with a comprehensive set of proposals to reform the congressional budget process. The general set of procedures proposed eventually was enacted into law, but certain of its aspects were unacceptable to other parts of the Congress. Thus the proposals were modified to accommodate congressional power centers that felt threatened by some of the initial provisions.

Support for budget reform in the House and Senate was virtually universal. Members of Congress wanted to restore the congressional power of the purse. Liberals wanted to counter President Nixon's impoundment of funds for social programs. And conservatives, including President Nixon, wanted Congress to discipline itself and cut spending. Thus those supporting the 1974 Budget Act resembled the coalition of reformers and fiscal conservatives who passed the Budget and Accounting Act of 1921.[1] That act, however, was intended to give greater budgetary power to the president. The 1974 act was intended to limit that spending power, which had increased so greatly in the intervening half century.

Although the primary impetus for budget reform came from the presidential threat to the congressional purse power, the final provisions of the act were shaped by the interplay of the fiscal power centers within the Congress. With any major change in procedures some power relationships will be affected; however, in order for the act to be passed it could not drastically threaten anyone's turf. The Joint Study Committee's proposal, along with the compromises and changes necessary for final passage, will now be considered as the legislative history of the act is traced.

The Legislative History of H.R. 7130

With the major problems delineated in the interim report, the Joint Study Committee went to work and came out with its final report on April 18, 1973.[2] The report contained a series of specific proposals meant to remedy the problems it had listed in its interim report. The membership of the committee was drawn primarily from the appropriations and revenue committees of the two houses (twenty-eight of thirty-two members). Thus one might expect that its recommendations would reflect the interests of the spending and revenue committees.[3] Consequently, many proposals of the Joint Study Committee, such as budget committee membership, the type of backdoor spending controls, and the firmness of initial spending ceilings, would subsequently be altered to make them acceptable to the rest of the Congress. But the overall scheme of the proposals was left intact in the final bill. The most striking aspect of the overall budget reform proposals was the fact that the existing budgetary process was not discarded and no congressional committee would lose an important component of its jurisdiction. Rather, the reformed budgetary process was layered over the existing system.[4] The Joint Study Committee's recommendations came out in identical form as H.R. 7130 and S. 1641, and were introduced on April 18, 1973.

The Joint Study Committee proposed to create special budget committees in both houses to review the president's budget proposals from an overall perspective. The House committee would have twenty-one members and the Senate, fifteen. One-third of the membership of each committee would come from the appropriations committees, one-third from the respective revenue committees, and one-third from the memberships at large. The report emphasized that existing committees would not be replaced. Chairmanships of the committees would rotate among members from the appropriations and revenue committees. There would be a joint professional staff to assist the committees.

The two budget committees would be responsible for reporting to their houses concurrent resolutions at the beginning of each session. These resolutions would provide limitations on overall budget outlays and new budget authority. They would also provide for appropriate levels of revenue and public debt. They would set ceilings for spending in categories that corresponded to the appropriations sub-committees' jurisdictions.[5] Such a proposal was a threat to the traditional discretion of the appropriations committees. If the new budget committees set subceilings on spending, their traditional flexibility would be limited. Yet the subceilings provision was a unanimous recommendation of the Joint Study Committee.[6]

Amendments to the resolutions would be allowed to provide flexibility but they would be out of order unless a "rule of consistency" was followed.[7] That is, any proposal to increase spending had to include a proposal to decrease spending elsewhere. Thus Congress would be bound by its formulation made six months before the fiscal year was to begin. A series of procedural rules was also proposed to help enforce the resolutions.

The proposed reforms would not affect existing backdoor spending but they would require that all future permanent appropriations go through the appropriations committees and that other backdoor spending limit payments to levels set by appropriations bills. This, of course, would enhance the power of the appropriations committees in relation to the legislative committees.

The above is an outline of the major aspects of the Joint Study Committee's proposals for budget reform. As has been noted, the makeup of the committee was weighted in favor of the spending and revenue committees and in the view of some, the bill represented their interests. Hence, for reasons of self-protection and for the purpose of improving the procedure, many amendments were proposed before budget reform was finally enacted into law. The next section traces the development of the legislation as it was managed by the committees and on the floors of the two houses.

The House

H.R. 7130 was referred to the Rules Committee, which is heavily influenced by the Democratic leadership in the House. Thus the committee could be expected to report out a bill with broad appeal to the body as a whole.[8] Richard Bolling took charge of the budget reform bill and resolved to put together an acceptable package. However, in order to do this he had to be careful to allay the fears of both liberals and conservatives. Support from both sides of the spectrum was necessary not only to pass the initial legislation, but also to ensure support for the process once it was enacted. Part of the reason the 1946 budget reform foundered was that it was perceived as a partisan measure.

First, the powerful House committee fiefdoms had to be assured that their prerogatives would not be eroded by the new act. In Bolling's mind two changes were necessary to allay their fears: the rigid spending ceilings of the Joint Study Committee would have to be modified, and the new budget committee could not be seen to usurp the traditional powers of the Appropriations Committee. Therefore, the Rules Committee version provided that Congress would set initial spending targets rather than rigid ceilings for budget authority and outlays. Congress would be able to change its initial decisions, if changing conditions warranted it. The other concession to traditional committee prerogatives was the decision to formulate the spending targets by way of functional subtotals (such as national defense, agriculture, health, etc.). The Joint Study Committee's proposal would have kept the subtotals in categories corresponding to appropriations bills. This, of course, would have presented the Appropriations Committee with the threat of having its decisions made by the new budget committee. The breakdown into functional categories would also allow Congress to focus its debate on spending priorities and make more conscious tradeoffs.[9]

Bolling also had to allay the liberals' suspicion of the reform proposals. They felt that the measure was loaded in favor of fiscal conservatives and that social programs would become victims of spending cuts. In response it was proposed that one-half, rather than two-thirds, of the budget committee membership would come from the fiscally conservative Appropriations and Way and Means Committees. In addition, all Democratic members of the budget committee in the House would be chosen by the democratic caucus rather than by the fiscal committees. The chairman would be chosen by the budget committee itself and would not have to be a member of the spending or revenue committees. Thus membership on the committee would be more likely to reflect the makeup of the whole House rather than the members of the more fiscally conservative committees.

Liberal interests were also reflected by the inclusion of an antiimpoundment measure that would enable Congress to restore many of the Nixon cuts in social programs. Fiscal conservatives were reassured by the decision to let stand the Joint Study Committee's provision to eliminate back door spending, which had been an increasingly vexatious thorn in the side of the Appropriations Committee. The whole House went along with the Rules Committee recommendations, and passed H.R. 7130 by 386 to 23 on December 5, 1973.

The Senate

The Senate Government Operations Committee, chaired by Sam Ervin, had original jurisdiction over the budget reform proposals and began to consider S. 1541, a modified version of S. 1641, which was the Joint Study Committee's proposal. The Subcommittee on Budgeting, Management, and Expenditures (with Lee Metcalf as chairman) initially considered the bill in April 1973 and recommended some compromises. One of these was to remove the quotas for members of the budget committee from the spending and revenue committees. It also favored establishing a Congressional Office of the Budget that would serve the whole Congress rather than be a joint staff for the budget committees.[10] As in the House, the major point of contention was the nature of the initial ceilings, that is, whether they would be firm ceilings or spending targets that could be modified.

A compromise was agreed upon that was made firm in the full committee and the bill was reported out on November 28,

1973. It would retain a firm ceiling on overall spending in the budget resolution but allow flexibility in subceiling targets. The final committee version contained no impoundment provisions and changed the timetable from the original version. S. 1541 was then referred to the Senate Committee on Rules and Administration at the insistence of Senator Robert Byrd.[11]

The Senate Rules Committee consciously made an attempt to take into account all major interests within the Senate in order to mold a bill that was both passable and workable.[12] Liberals argued that under the Government Operations Committee's version of S. 1541, when it came around to reconciling all of the separate appropriations bills with the original targets, the tendency would be to cut spending for social programs.[13] Accordingly, the Senate Rules Committee called for a second budget resolution before final action. This would allow Congress to revise its original targets upward and compensate by means of a tax increase or larger deficit along with, or instead of, spending cuts. The previous timetable for budget actions was also modified.

Two other compromises affected the power of the appropriations committees. The Senate Rules' version loosened the requirements on backdoor spending slightly, thereby allowing the legislative committees to retain some of their spending authority. Appropriations action would still be necessary for contract and loan authority, but primary authority for entitlement programs would remain outside the appropriations process. They would, however, be referred to the appropriations committee that could recommend a provision limiting entitlement outlays. But the Byrd compromise also made a concession to the Appropriations Committee. The target totals initially recommended by the budget committees would be broken down into functional categories, rather than the administrative categories that correspond to appropriation subcommittees. This would give the Appropriations Committee more flexibility in deciding how to allocate funds.[14]

Conference and Final Provisions

The conference committee[15] met between April and June

1974 in order to iron out the differences between S. 1541 and H.R. 7130 and to put the budget reform package in final form. The Conference Report filed on June 12 reflected the fact that, with the exception of impoundment control, there were no major differences between the final versions of the two houses.[16] There were, however, major differences with the original Joint Study Committee's proposal. Most of these differences were worked out in House and Senate committee consideration as described above, and were not issues in conference. According to Representative Richard Bolling: "Although the Joint Study Committee set the overall framework for budget reform legislation, it provided a rigid and probably unworkable set of procedures."[17] Specifically, it set rigid initial spending totals and made no provision for impoundment control. The following section will briefly describe the Congressional Budget and Impoundment Control Act of 1974, with emphases on House-Senate differences and the changes in the traditional budgetary process.

According to the managers of the bill in the House and Senate, the purpose of the act was to "assure congressional budget control; provide for the congressional determination of the appropriate level of Federal revenues and expenditures; provide a system of impoundment control; establish national budget priorities; and provide for the furnishing of information to Congress by the executive branch."[18] This, in turn, was to "return to Congress the power and responsibility of the purse."[19] To accomplish these tasks the act set up a new congressional budgetary process. The act itself is divided into ten titles that can be grouped into four categories: (1) Titles I and II establish budget committees in the House and Senate and a Congressional Budget Office to provide the Congress with the analytical resources needed to examine alternatives to the president's budget; (2) Titles III and IV set up a new series of budget procedures and a timetable to guide their execution; (3) Titles V through IX establish a new fiscal year, improved budget terminology and information for the president's budget, better evaluation and review of federal programs, and the dates upon which the act became effective; and (4) Title X provides procedures to control impoundments.

The budget committees set up under the act (Title I)

consisted of twenty-three members in the House and fifteen in the Senate. The House committee has a rotating membership with five from Appropriations and Ways and Means Committees,two from House leadership, and eleven at-large members.[20]The ratio of money committee members to others represents a more "liberal"(less fiscally conservative) ratio than that of earlier forms of the bill. The function of the budget committees is to report to their respective houses "concurrent resolutions," which are described below. These resolutions are intended to provide a means by which Congress can set national fiscal policy through the determination of levels of total spending, revenue, and national debt. The focus of the two committees is the implementation of macroeconomic policy through the budget, which no other one committee has done in the past. The committee is also to choose among competing budgetary priorities.

There was a conscious decision that the new committees would overlay the traditional budgetary process and not replace it. Senator Javits told the Senate Budget Committee that "under no circumstances should we be considered competitive with or duplicative of the Appropriations Committee."[21] It was necessary to minimize the threat to existing power centers in Congress in order to pass the reform bill at all. The final form of the bill is a masterpiece of changing procedures in an important way without challenging existing power centers.

The Congressional Budget Office (CBO) (Title II) is headed by a director who is appointed by the speaker of the House and president pro tempore of the Senate and has a term of four years. It is the duty of CBO to provide Congress with information and analysis concerning the president's budget and to report on alternative sets of priorities. It also does "scorekeeping," that is, it keeps track of congressional appropriations measures and relates them to the budget targets established in the concurrent resolutions. The Congressional Budget Office is intended to be a nonpartisan agency and to provide the Congress with the capability of making independent budget estimates and economic projections in order to make Congress less dependent on executive branch data and analyses.[22]

The new budget process established by the act begins with the fiscal year on October 1. The change from July 1 was intended to give Congress three more months to consider the budget, since the president still would deliver his budget proposal in January. On November 10 the president begins the budget cycle by submitting a current services budget, which will estimate the budget resources necessary to continue existing federal operations under certain economic assumptions.

Fifteen days after Congress convenes, the President submits his budget to Congress and by March 15 all congressional committees submit reports to the budget committees regarding any budgetary matters pertinent to their responsibilities. This is a procedure intended to give the budget committee guidance in proposing the concurrent resolution. By April 1 the Congressional Budget Office is to submit to the budget committees its analysis of the president's budget and possible alternatives to it.

By April 15 the two budget committees are to report the first concurrent resolution to their houses. The concurrent resolution is a device by which Congress can set overall levels for federal fiscal policy and use these for guidance in formulating a congressional budget. The concurrent resolution will set appropriate levels for total budget authority, outlays, federal revenues, surplus or deficit, and the public debt. In the original version of H.R. 7130 these totals were to be firm ceilings that would bind Congress for the fiscal year. It appeared, however, that such a bill was unlikely to pass. Congress did not want to lock itself into a budget that could not take changing economic conditions into account. Consequently the bill was changed so that the original totals would be targets that could be changed by subsequent concurrent resolutions.

These budget totals are subdivided into functional categories that do not correspond to the appropriations bills reported by appropriations subcommittees. This is in line with the intent of the conference committee: the budget committees should be concerned with broad issues of budget priorities and fiscal policy rather than particular programs and agencies.[23] The decision to use functional rather than administrative categories was designed to protect the prerogatives of the appropriations committees, giving them more flexibility to allocate the budgetary subtotals.²⁴ The appropriations committees are expected to stay within the totals set for the functional categories, but they can decide how to allocate the total among dfferent programs.

On or before May 15 Congress is to consider the budget committees' reports and adopt its first concurrent budget resolution. Also by this date all legislation authorizing new budget authority is to be reported by the legislative committees. The above two deadlines must be met so that the appropriations committees will be able to act within the confines of authorizing legislation and in light of the budget targets set by the concurrent resolution. After May 15 the appropriations committees proceed to examine spending bills as they have in the past, but with guidance from the first concurrent resolution.

By the seventh day after Labor Day all action on new budget authority is to be completed and by September 15 the second concurrent resolution is to be passed. The purpose of the second resolution is to enable Congress to take into account any changes in economic conditions or programmatic needs. By September 25 the second resolution is to be implemented by adjusting the spending, revenue, and debt legislation to be in conformity with it. Once this is done no legislation may be considered that violates the resolution by increasing expenditures above total budget authority or reducing revenues below the level set in the resolution. If deemed necessary, however, Congress could pass a subsequent concurrent resolution revising the totals, though it must stay within the confines of the latest resolution.

Thus the act does not set rigid spending provisions that may not be changed; it merely provides a mechanism by which any changes have to be made consciously and deliberately. One committee can no longer increase spending without regard to other parts of the budget. The whole Congress will have to decide on changes to the resolution. On the other hand, if Congress does not wish to hold spending down or act with fiscal wisdom, there is nothing that can make it do so.

Backdoor Spending

In addition to the new budget process, the 1974 Budget Act

also set up new provisions limiting backdoor spending. Backdoor spending, as mentioned in Chapter 3, is legislation that creates budget authority but originates in a legislative rather than appropriations committee. The House version of H.R. 7130 would have ended all backdoor spending. The Senate version, however, had somewhat looser strictures and it prevailed. The new act provides that all contract and borrowing authority granted to government agencies can only be provided to the extent that the funds are also provided in appropriations acts. This closes the backdoor by which such authority could be enacted in the past by legislative committees without having to run the gauntlet of the appropriations committees.

Entitlement authority, which provides funds to persons who qualify for them under the provisions of the law, is now subject to the reconciliation process. Decisions about the scope of the legislation would remain with the legislative committee involved. Proposed entitlement legislation, however, would be referred to the appropriations committee before floor consideration. The referral would have a fifteen-day limit and would apply only to entitlements in excess of budget resolution totals. It would allow the appropriations committee to propose an amendment limiting the funds provided.

Exempted from the backdoor provisions are social security trust funds, 90 percent self-financed trust funds, government corporations, and general revenue sharing legislation. The final compromise between the House and Senate represents a slight pull back from the original Joint Study Committee proposal. The act as a whole dilutes the authority of the appropriations committees by making them subject to the totals proposed by the new budget committees. Appropriations did, however, get back some of the authority they had lost to the legislative committees over the years through their use of backdoor spending. The more fiscally conservative House would have given it all back, but the final version made special provisions for entitlements.[25]

Impoundment

The major compromise that grew out of the conference on the budget bill involved the impoundment provisions of Title

X. The House version of H.R. 7130 included the substance of H.R. 8480, which would have allowed the president to withhold funds unless one house disapproved. The Senate version deleted the "other developments" phrase from the Antideficiency Act but did not include its more general antiimpoundment legislation. The conference compromise included a combination of the provisions of H.R. 8480 and S. 373, previously proposed legislation intended to limit impoundment.

Previous antiimpoundment legislation had not passed in part because some congressmen had felt that Congress had been acting fiscally irresponsibly and needed to put its own house in order. Conversely, the conference committee felt that enacting budget reforms without limiting impoundment would be futile. In the words of Richard Bolling:

> It makes no sense for Congress to establish new procedures for the appropriation of funds if the President can override the will of Congress by means of impoundment. At the same time, the methods used to control Presidential impoundments must be reasonable and appropriate. They should neither deny the President the capability to manage the executive branch nor impose upon Congress the burden of redoing its previous decisions.[26]

Title X of the 1974 Budget Act provides two procedures for controlling impoundments. If the president determines that all of the budget authority provided will not be necessary to carry out a program, or that fiscal reasons necessitate the withholding of budget authority, or that budget authority provided for a single year should be reserved from obligation that year, he must transmit to Congress a special message requesting the rescission of such funds. Congress must act affirmatively on the rescission message within forty-five days or the funds must be released. If the president withholds funds for any other reason, he must transmit to Congress a deferral message. If at any time after this transmittal either house of Congress passes an "impoundment resolution" the president must release the funds.

The comptroller general has the authority to review each presidential message in order to determine if it conforms to the provisions of the act. If he finds that a message has been misclassified, he is directed to make a report to Congress. If he finds that the president has failed to report a reservation or deferral, he is to make a report to the Congress, and the report will have the same effect as if it were a message from the president. If the president fails to comply with the provisions of the act dealing with the release of funds, the comptroller general is empowered to go to court to seek their release.

The passage of the 1974 Budget Act was the result of a broad-based coalition. Support within the Congress was nearly universal, as is reflected in the final floor votes for passage: 75-0 in the Senate and 401-6 in the House. Support for reform came from several directions and for various reasons that are not necessarily mutually exclusive. Conservatives had long sought some method of limiting federal spending and particularly of reducing the national debt. They felt that the new Budget Act could help achieve these aims by forcing members of Congress to vote on the size of the deficit or surplus and put ceilings on spending categories. Liberals had hopes that the new budget committees would limit the influence of the fiscally conservative appropriations and revenue committees. They also wanted to stop the damage that impoundment was doing to many social programs.

There was institutional support from members of the appropriations committees who wanted to end backdoor spending, which kept a large percentage of the budget from their purview. There was also a desire in many parts of Congress to bring spending "under control" by making a larger portion of the budget subject to change in any one fiscal year without reversing existing legislation. Finally, there was the feeling that Congress ought to recover the power of the purse, which had been slipping to the executive branch since 1921. This attitude was shared by liberals and conservatives, Democrats and Republicans, and was intensified by other aspects of the "imperial presidency," described in Chapter 6.

The feeling that the executive branch had overstepped its bounds was shared by most members of the supporting coalition.

Notes

1. For the floor debates surrounding passage of S. 1541 and H.R. 7130, see U.S., Congress, House, *Congressional Record,* 4 December 1973 (daily ed.), pp. H10671-720; 19 March 1974 (daily ed.), pp. S3831-65.

2. U.S., Congress, House, Joint Study Committee on Budget Control, *Recommendations for Improving Congressional Control Over Budgetary Outlay and Receipt Totals,* 18 April 1973, H. Rept. 7130.

3. See Allen Schick, "Budget Reform Legislation: Reorganizing Congressional Centers of Fiscal Power," *Harvard Journal on Legislation* 11, no. 2 (February 1974):303 at 317.

4. See ibid., p. 319.

5. See Joint Study Committee, *Improving Congressional Control,* p. 3.

6. Schick, "Budget Reform Legislation," p. 318.

7. See Joint Study Committee, *Improving Congressional Control,* p. 5.

8. Schick, "Budget Reform Legislation," p. 320.

9. Joel Havemann, *Congress and the Budget* (Bloomington: Indiana University Press, 1978), pp. 30-31. See also Democratic Study Group Fact Sheet, "Budget and Impoundment Control Act of 1973," no. 93-12 (26 November 1973): 21-23. Havemann's book contains an excellent analysis of the initial experience with the new budget act and its impact on the Congress.

10. See Schick, "Budget Reform Legislation," p. 324.

11. Congressional Quarterly, *1973 Almanac* (Washington D.C., Congressional Quarterly, Inc., 1974), p. 252. See also Schick, "Budget Reform Legislation," p. 325.

12. See *Congressional Quarterly Weekly Report* 32, no. 7 (February 16, 1974):378; and *Congressional Quarterly Weekly Report* 32, no. 8 (23 February 1974):514.

13. Ibid., p. 378.

14. See Democratic Study Group Fact Sheet, "Budget and Impoundment Control Act of 1973," pp. 21-23 for pros and cons of the functional category breakdown. See also *Congressional Quarterly*

Weekly Report 32, no. 11 (16 March 1974):679-81.

15. Members of the conference committee were: Senators Sam J. Ervin, Jr., Edmund S. Muskie; Abraham Ribicoff; Lee Metcalf; Howard W. Cannon; Clairborne Pell; Robert Brock; M.W. Cook; Hugh Scott; and Robert P. Griffin; Representatives Richard Bolling; Bernie Sisk; John Young; Gillis W. Long; Dave Martin; Delbert Latta; and Del Clawson.

16. U.S., Congress, Senate, Conference Committee, *Conference Report*, 12 June 1974, S. Rept. 93-924.

17. U.S., Congress, House, *Congressional Record*, 18 June 1974 (daily ed.), p. H5180.

18. U.S., Congress, Senate, Conference Committee, Conference Report, 12 June 1974, 93-924, p. 49.

19. U.S., Congress, House, *Congressional Record*, 18 June 1974 (daily ed.), p. H5180.

20. Now amended to twenty-five and sixteen members, respectively, and thirteen at-large members in the House. U.S., Congress, House, *Congressional Record*, 14 January 1975 (daily ed.), 121, p. H5, and 17 January 1975 (daily ed.), 121, p. S511.

21. Quoted in *Congressional Quarterly Weekly Report* 32, no. 36 (September 7, 1974):2418.

22. See Joel Havemann,"House, Senate disagree on director for the Budget Office," *National Journal* 6, no. 52 (December 28, 1974):1960.

23. See U.S., Congress, House, *Congressional Record*, 18 June 1974 (daily ed.), p. H5180.

24. See Democratic Study Group Fact Sheet, "Budget and Impoundment Control Act of 1973," pp. 21-23.

25. For an explanation of Title VI of the act covering backdoor spending, see *Congressional Quarterly Weekly Report* 32, no. 24 (June 15, 1974):1593. See also U.S., Congress, House, *Congressional Record*, 18 June 1974 (daily ed.), p. H5182.

26. U.S., Congress, House, *Congressional Record*, 18 June 1974 (daily ed.), p. H5182.

8
Conclusion

In the 1970s the Congress, in order to obtain a greater voice in national policy-making vis-à-vis the president, tried to reassert itself in several different areas. Foremost among the disputes with the presidency were the areas of foreign affairs, war powers, and the budgetary process. The impeachment proceedings fit into this context of congressional resurgence, but were the result of the special circumstances of Watergate. The judiciary was a major factor in the checking of presidential assertions of power. Court decisions in the areas of executive privilege and impoundment have made significant differences in the political context in which the president has had to operate. This book has examined the struggle between the president and Congress over fiscal power. It has been concluded that the impoundment controversy was the major factor in the reassertion of congressional budget power through the 1974 Budget Act.

Several important questions have been raised and remain to be dealt with. One of them is the question of timing. There has been a major reform of the budgetary process, the most important change since the Budget and Accounting Act of 1921. Why did this major event occur in 1974 and not at some other time? There is also a problem in trying to distinguish partisan political conflict from an institutional conflict between the president and Congress. Can these two factors be disentangled? Finally, some implications for the separation of powers system are drawn.

Major Factors Causing Change in 1974

Previous attempts at budget reform have occurred in 1921 and 1946. The Budget and Accounting Act of 1921 established an executive budget in order to bring spending under the coherent control of one decision maker who would be held accountable by the Congress. Section 138 of the Legislative Reorganization Act of 1946 called for a legislative budget. Its inclusion in the act resulted in part from a desire by the Republican Congress to thwart President Truman. The 1974 Budget Act resulted in part from partisan motives and in part from a desire to improve congressional budget procedures, but we must look further in order to explain why it occurred in 1974.

The development of the 1974 Budget Act was more closely involved with the institutional clash between Congress and the presidency than the two earlier reforms. The internal problems meant to be remedied by the 1974 reform, such as fragmentation of spending power and lack of one coherent budgetary perspective, had been problems in Congress for most of the century, so any explanation of the timing of the act must deal with external factors affecting the Congress, that is, the institutional and political conflicts with the president.

The external factors that contributed to the passage of the Budget Act in 1974 can be divided into three categories: (1) general tensions that existed between the president and Congress, (2) the political style of President Nixon, and (3) the institutional clash between Congress and the executive branch over the spending power. These factors have been dealt with throughout previous chapters. The arguments are summarized below in the above order and the position is taken that the institutional clash was most important.

Due to the constitutional structure of the government and the sharing of the spending power by the president and Congress, there has been a tension between the two branches that many times became focused in the budgetary arena. These institutional tensions were exacerbated when the president and Congress were of different parties. For the most part, the Republican and Democratic parties espouse differing policy priorities, and this includes attitudes toward fiscal policy. Therefore, when President Nixon was elected at the same time the Democratic majority was returned to Congress, there were bound to be clashes. President Nixon saw himself as a fiscal conservative who was elected in part to hold down federal spending. He pressed this policy preference, particularly with respect to many of the social programs enacted under President Lyndon Johnson's Great Society program. This would obviously irritate Democratic members of Congress, many of whom had passed Great Society legislation several years earlier. During President Nixon's terms these partisan conflicts, when combined with the president's political style and his use of impoundment, led to a crisis in interbranch relations.

Although it is difficult to deal precisely with presidential personality or style, it is a general observation that President Nixon approached Congress many times with an attitude of confrontation rather than accommodation. President Nixon's actions with regard to impoundment were in this general pattern. He seldom consulted with congressional leaders about questions of impoundment. This was in contrast to President Lyndon Johnson, who impounded funds at significant levels but who was careful not to provoke a constitutional crisis. An important symbolic gesture was President Nixon's claim that he had the constitutional power to impound funds. Considering the disputed status of impoundment at the time, such a claim was considered confrontational.

The above two categories of factors affected the timing of the 1974 Budget Act. The most important set of factors, however, was the institutional threat by the presidency to the congressional power of the purse. All of the factors were intertwined, but this last issue can be meaningfully distinguished. The two major components were the increase of the formal powers of the presidency over the budgetary process and the manner in which President Nixon used the impoundment power. These threats were enhanced by his declaration that the president has the constitutional right to impound funds.

During the second term of Richard Nixon the formal institutional control of the executive branch over the budgetary process was greater than it had ever been before. At the same time that presidential control over the budget was greatest, presidential impoundment of appropriated funds was also at its peak. This is true both in quantity and types of impoundment. If the president could refuse to spend funds for purposes he did not approve, it would amount to an item veto. And if the Congress could not compel spending, the president would have an absolute veto over appropriations. Hence the escalation of the quantity and quality of impoundments during the Nixon administration combined with the formal powers of the Office of Management and Budget to present the Congress with a serious threat to its control over spending. It was this threat that precipitated congressional reaction in 1974.

The Problem of Distinguishing Institutional from Partisan Conflict

Although the clashes between President Nixon and the Congress in the early 1970s had an important partisan component, the shift in domestic policy priorities had important implications for the power of Congress as an institution. The president was thought to be overstepping his constitutional bounds by shifting priorities through impounding funds. In addition to his actions he made a formal claim that his impoundments were a constitutional power of the president. Hence, President Nixon was not only trying to win short term political battles with the Congress over fiscal priorities, but he was also making long term claims about the formal powers of the presidency.

The contention of this book is that it was the combination of partisan and institutional factors that brought about the reassertion of congressional budgetary power through court decisions and legislative action. It might be argued, however, that the partisan element was overwhelming: instead of Congress reacting against an increasingly powerful presidency, the Democratic party through its majority in Congress was trying to implement its policy priorities by undercutting presidential spending power. The argument of this book, however, is that in addition to the partisan clash there was another important component—a threat to Congress as an institution—that contributed to the resolution of the controversy through a reassertion of congressional power. There are three points to support this conclusion: (1) any clash over basic powers has institutional implications, (2) major votes in Congress reflect bipartisan support for antiimpoundment legislation, and (3) the actions of the judiciary indicate that more than partisan politics was involved.

Aside from partisan political factors, if the presidency and the Congress are controlled by different parties, a battle over as basic a power as the spending power has implications for the balance of institutional powers. If the president from one party can prevail over a Congress dominated by the other party when there is a basic disagreement, the relative powers of the two institutions are biased toward the president in that area. Consequently, when President Nixon claimed the constitutional power to impound funds despite the wishes of Congress, the implications for congressional spending power were more than a Republican victory. Unless that claim was repudiated, any incumbent of the presidency would have the same power.

Another way that the distinction can be made between partisan and institutional factors in budget reform is to look at voting in the Congress on antiimpoundment bills. The major antiimpoundment bills that were considered in Congress were Senate Bill S. 373 and House Bill H.R. 7130. By August 1973 the Senate and the House had passed these antiimpoundment bills but they never became law because the two houses could not agree to a common set of procedures. The pressure to pass an antiimpoundment bill was alleviated at that time because the courts had begun to accept cases, and decisions were being made against the administration. Both houses, however, overwhelmingly passed their own versions of the Congressional Budget and Impoundment Control Act: S. 1541 passed the Senate, 80-0; and H.R. 7130 passed the House, 386-23. In June the final version of the 1974 Budget Act was passed, Title X of which contained procedures that were a combination of the antiimpoundment procedures proposed in the two bills. The fact that both houses had passed antiimpoundment bills indicates that there was an institutionally perceived threat to congressional spending power. Furthermore, the fact that the

1974 Budget Act passed the Congress with virtually no opposition indicates that this perception was not merely a function of partisan differences.

In addition to the above two factors, the actions of the courts in impoundment litigation indicate that the issue was more than a partisan dispute between Republicans and Democrats. This is not to assert that the courts are not affected by partisan politics, but the near unanimity of judicial decisions indicates that the courts were acting under very similar perceptions of the legal status of the president's actions, which led them to decide virtually all cases against the president's claims to impoundment powers. In the Supreme Court case, *Train* v. *New York City,* there were no dissents from the decision against the government, despite the presence of four Nixon appointees.

The response of the judiciary to the litigation growing out of the impoundment controversy was an affirmation of the congressional perception that the president was encroaching in an important way on the congressional spending power. The judiciary was performing its constitutional function, and its near unanimity lends support to the position that there was more going on in the impoundment controversy than partisan politics.

Implications for Interbranch Interactions

The checks and balances of the separation of powers system were operating in the struggle over the purse power. Abuses of the budgetary power by the Congress at the end of the nineteenth century led to delegation of more power to the president through the executive budget. This delegation led to increasingly centralized control of the budget in the Budget Bureau. This, combined with executive use of impoundment, led Congress to reassert itself in the 1974 Budget Act.

The judiciary also moved to check the president, and it is significant that the courts had not been active in the budgetary process before the impoundment cases. Neither had the courts been often willing to compel executive action. Yet the Supreme Court affirmed a decision ordering the director of the Environmental Protection Agency to allot certain funds that the president had ordered him not to allot. In this manner, the judiciary aligned itself with the Congress in checking power concentrated in the presidency. It is doubtful that court cases defining legal rights and duties are the best way to make political and administrative decisions about spending. However, given the context of confrontation between the president and Congress over impoundment, the courts performed an important function of arbitration. They provided the legitimacy of the legal system for the resolution of the dispute by refusing to uphold the president's claimed right to impound funds.

This book has dealt with the checking of the presidency by Congress and the courts in the budgetary arena; however, there may be a general trend of which the budget power was only one facet. Congress also reacted to concentrated power—what it perceived to be the abuse of power—in the presidency when it passed the War Power Resolution in 1973. It tried to limit presidential discretion in foreign affairs through the Jackson Amendment. It tried to make executive information more accessible through the Freedom of Information Act. Most strikingly, the House pursued its impeachment inquiry against President Nixon to the point where he was forced to resign or suffer probable impeachment and conviction.

In recent years the courts have also been aligned against certain uses of presidential power, at times in response to litigation by members of Congress. The courts struck down Nixon's unprecedented use of the pocket veto. They enjoined the dismantling of the Office of Economic Opportunity by the executive. They refused to uphold President Nixon's interpretation of the executive privilege doctrine. And they have enforced various laws against former high executive branch officials in prosecutions resulting from Watergate-related events.

These reactions of Congress and the courts came in the context of a historical trend of increasingly centralized power in the presidency. Many of them, moreover, came during the administration of Richard Nixon. This book has argued that there was a general breakdown in comity between the two branches during the Nixon administration and that his impoundment actions were a major cause of the 1974 Budget Act. The other two branches have been sensitized to the potential for the abuse of power in the executive branch.

Future presidents can expect that Congress and the courts will be more active than they have been in the past in protecting their perceived institutional prerogatives against expansive presidential actions.

Selected Bibliography

Books

Baily, Stephen Kemp. *Congress Makes a Law*. New York: Random House, 1950.

Bolling, Richard. *Power in the House*. New York: Capricorn Books, 1974.

Brown, Richard E. *The GAO*. Knoxville: University of Tennessee Press, 1970.

Browne, Vincent J. *The Control of the Public Budget*. Washington, D.C.: Public Affairs Press, 1949.

Brundage, Percival Flack. *The Bureau of the Budget*. New York: Praeger, 1970.

Burkhead, Jesse. *Government Budgeting*. New York: John Wiley and Sons, Inc., 1956.

Corwin, Edward S. *The President*. New York: New York University Press, 1957.

Dawes, Charles G. *The First Year of the Budget of the United States*. New York: Harper and Brothers, 1923.

Fenno, Richard. *The Power of the Purse*. Boston: Little, Brown and Co., 1966.

Fisher, Louis. *President and Congress*. New York: The Free Press, 1972.

Fisher, Louis. *Presidential Spending Power*. Princeton, N.J.: Princeton University Press, 1975.

Galloway, George B. *The Legislative Process in Congress*. New York: Thomas Y. Crowell Co., 1955.

Harris, Joseph P. *Congressional Control of Administration*.

Washington, D.C.: Brookings Institution, 1964.

Havemann, Joel. *Congress and the Budget.* Bloomington: Indiana University Press, 1978.

Mansfield, Harvey C. *The Comptroller General.* New Haven, Conn.: Yale University Press, 1939.

Neustadt, Richard W. *Presidential Power.* New York: John Wiley and Sons, Inc., 1960.

Sharkansky, Ira. *The Politics of Taxing and Spending.* New York: Bobbs-Merrill Co., Inc., 1969.

Smithies, Arthur. *The Budgetary Process in the United States.* New York: McGraw-Hill, 1955.

Tugwell, Rexford G. *The Enlargement of the Presidency.* New York: Doubleday, 1960.

Wallace, Robert Ash. *Congressional Control of Federal Spending.* Detroit, Mich.: Wayne State University Press, 1960.

Weidenbaum, Murray L., and Saloma, John S. *Congress and the Federal Budget.* Washington, D.C.: American Enterprise Institute, 1965.

Wildavsky, Aaron. *Budgeting.* Boston: Little, Brown, and Co., 1975.

Wildavsky, Aaron. *The Politics of the Budgetary Process.* 2nd ed. Boston: Little, Brown, and Co., 1974.

Wilmerding, Lucius Jr. *The Spending Power.* New Haven, Conn.: Yale University Press, 1943.

Articles

Archer, Warren J. "Presidential Impounding of Funds: The Judicial Response." *Chicago Law Review* 40:328.

Baade, Hans W. "Mandatory Appropriations of Public Funds: A Comparative Study, Part I." *Virginia Law Review* 60:393.

Boggs, Hale. "Executive Impoundment of Congressionally Appropriated Funds." *University of Florida Law Review* 24: 221.

Burkhead, Jesse V. "Federal Budgetary Developments: 1947-48." *Public Administration Review* 8:267.

Burkhead, Jesse, and Charles Knerr. "Congressional Budget Reform: New Decision Structures." Paper presented at the Conference on Federal Fiscal Responsibility, Society for Public Choice, March, 1976.

Ellwood, John W., and James A. Thurber. "The New Congressional Budget Process: Its Causes, Consequences, and Possible Success." Paper presented at the Symposium on Legislative Reform and Public Policy, Lincoln, Nebraska, March, 1976.

Ellwood, John W., and James A. Thurber. "The New Congressional Budget Process in the House of Representatives: Some Hypotheses." Paper presented at the Southwest Political Science Association Convention, April, 1976.

Fielder, Clinton. "Reform of the Congressional Legislative Budget," *National Tax Journal* 4:65.

Fisher, Louis. "Congress, the Executive and the Budget." *The Annals* 411:102.

Fisher, Louis. "Reprogramming of Funds by the Defense Department." *Journal of Politics* 36:77.

Galloway, George B. "The Operation of the Legislative Reorganization Act of 1946." *American Political Science Review* 45:41.

Georgetown Law Journal. "Presidential Impoundment: Constitutional Theories and Political Realities." Vol. 61, p. 1295.

Gilmour, Robert S. "Central Legislative Clearance: A Revised Perspective." *Public Administration Review* 31:150.

Green, Frederick. "Separation of Governmental Powers." *Yale Law Journal* 29:369.

Harvard Law Review. "Impoundment of Funds." Vol. 86, p. 1505.

Heclo, Hugh. "OMB and the Presidency—the problem of 'neutral competence'." *The Public Interest* (Winter 1975):80.

Iowa Law Review. "The Likely Law of Executive Impoundment." Vol. 59, p. 50.

Leiserson, Avery. "Coordination of Federal Budgetary and Appropriations Procedures Under the Legislative Reorganization Act of 1946." *National Tax Journal* 1:118.

Levinson, Harold L., and Jon L. Mills. "Budget Reform and Impoundment Control." *Vanderbilt Law Review* 27:615.

Levinson, Harold L., and Jon L. Mills. "Impoundment: A Search For Legal Principles." *University of Florida Law Review* 26:191.

Marx, Fritz Morstein. "The Bureau of the Budget: Its Evolution and Present Role." *American Political Science Review* 39: Part 1, p. 633; Part 2, p. 869.

Nelson, Dalmas H. "The Omnibus Appropriations Act of 1950." *Journal of Politics* 15:274.

Neustadt, Richard E. "The Constraining of the President: the Presidency after Watergate." *British Journal of Political Science* 4:383.

Neustadt, Richard E. "Presidency and Legislation: The Growth of Central Clearance." *American Political Science Review* 48:641.

Ohio State Law Journal. "Impoundment of Funds Appropriated by Congress." Vol. 34, p. 416.

Phillips, John. "The Hadacol of the Budget Makers." *National Tax Journal* 4:255.

Pine, Norman. "The Impoundment Dilemma: Crisis in Constitutional Government." *Yale Review of Law and Social Action* 3:99.

Pollak, Louis H., Charles L. Black, Jr., and Alexander M. Bickel. "The Congressional and Executive Roles in War-Making: An Analytical Framework." *Congressional Record* 116:16478.

Schick, Allen. "Budget Reform Legislation: Reorganizing Congressional Centers of Fiscal Power." *Harvard Journal on Legislation* 11:303.

Schick, Allen. "The Budget Bureau that Was: Thoughts on the Rise, Decline, and Future of a Presidential Agency." *Law and Contemporary Problems* (1974):519.

Stanton, Nile. "History and Practice of Executive Impoundment of Appropriated Funds." *Nebraska Law Review* 53:1.

Weinraub, Sally. "The Impoundment Question—An Overview." *Brooklyn Law Review* 40:342.

Yale Law Journal. "Protecting the Fisc: Executive Impoundment and Congressional Power." Vol. 82, p. 1636.

Government Documents

U.S., Library of Congress, Congressional Research Service, Allen Schick, analyst, *The Impoundment Control Act of 1974*, 31 January 1975, no. 75-27.

U.S., Library of Congress, Congressional Research Service, Allen Schick, analyst, *The First Years of the Congressional Budget Process*, 1976, no. 76-121S.

U.S., Library of Congress, Congressional Research Service, Allen Schick, analyst, *The Impoundment Control Act of 1974: Legislative History and Implementation*, 1976, no. 76-45S.

U.S., Library of Congress, Congressional Research Service, Louis Fisher, analyst, *Budget Concepts and Terminology: The Appropriations Phase*, 21 November 1974, no. 74-210.

U.S., Library of Congress, Congressional Research Service, Louis Fisher, analyst, *Court Cases on Impoundment of Funds*, 1974, no. 74-61.

U.S., Library of Congress, Congressional Research Service, Stuart Glass, analyst, *Presidential Impoundment of Congressionally Appropriated Funds: An Analysis of Recent Federal Court Decisions*, 25 March 1974, no. 74-82A.

U.S., Congress, House, Committee on the Judiciary, *Statement of Information*, Book 12, *Impoundment of Funds*, Impeachment Hearings, 93d Cong., 2d sess., May-June 1974.

U.S., Congress, House, Committee on Rules, *Impoundment Reporting and Review*, Hearings on H.R. 5193, 93d Cong., 1st sess., 1973.

U.S., Congress, Joint Committee on Congressional Operations, *Court Challenges to Executive Branch Impoundments of Appropriated Funds*, Special Report, 93d Cong., 2d sess., 1974.

U.S., Congress, Joint Study Committee on Budget Control, *Improving Congressional Budget Control*, Hearings, 93d Cong., 1st sess., 1973.

U.S., Congress, Senate, Ad Hoc Subcommittee on Impoundment of Funds of the Committee on Government Operations and the Subcommittee on Separation of Powers of the Committee on the Judiciary, *Impoundment of Appropriated*

Funds by the President, Joint Hearings on S.373, 93d Cong., 1st sess., 1973.

U.S., Congress, Senate, *Congressional Budget and Impoundment Control Act of 1974,* Conference Report to Accompany H.R. 7130, 93d Cong., 2d sess., 1974.

U.S., Congress, Senate, Committee of the Judiciary, Subcommittee on Separation of Powers, *Executive Impoundment of Appropriated Funds,* Hearings, 92d Cong., 1st sess., March 1971.

U.S., Congress, Senate, Subcommittee on Separation of Powers of the Committee on the Judiciary, *Separation of Powers and the Independent Agencies,* 91st Cong., 1st sess., 1969.

U.S., Congress, Senate, Committee on Government Operations, *Congressional Budget and Impoundment Control Act of 1974,* Legislative History of S. 1541 and H.R. 7130, 93rd Cong., 2d sess., 1974.

U.S., Congress, Senate, Subcommittee on Budgeting, Management and Expenditures, Committee on Government Operations, *Improving Congressional Control of the Budget.* Hearings, 93d Cong., 1st sess., 1973.

U.S., Congress, Senate, Subcommittee on Budgeting, Management and Expenditures of the Committee on Government Operations, *Improving Congressional Control Over the Budget, A Compendium of Materials,* 93d Cong., 1st sess., 1973.

U.S., Congress, Senate, Committee on Rules and Administration, *Congressional Budget Act of 1974,* Report to Accompany S.1541, 93d Cong., 2d sess., 1974.

U.S., Congress, Senate, Subcommittee on Standing Rules of the Senate of the Committee on Rules and Administration, *Federal Budget Control by the Congress,* Hearings, 93d Cong., 2d sess., 1974.

Court Cases

Baker v. *Carr.,* 369 U.S. 186 (1962).

Berends v. *Butz,* 357 F. Supp. 143 (D. Minn. 1973).

Brown v. *Ruckelshaus,* No. 73-154-AAH, consolidated with the *City of Los Angeles* v. *Ruckelshaus,* No. 73-736-AAH, 5

E.R.C. 1803 (C.D. Cal., Sept. 7, 1973).

Campaign Clean Water, Inc. v. *Train,* No. 73-1745 (4th Cir., Dec. 10, 1973); remanding *Campaign Clean Waters, Inc.* v. *Ruckelshaus,* 361 F. Supp. 689 (E.D. Va. 1973).

Citizens to Preserve Overton Park v. *Volpe,* 401 U.S. 402 (1971).

Citizens of New York v. *Train,* No. 73-1705 (D.C. Cir., Jan. 23, 1974), aff'g *City of New York* v. *Ruckelshaus,* 41 U.S.L.W. 2602 (D.D.C., May 8, 1973).

Dugan v. *Rank,* 372 U.S. 609 (1963).

Eisen v. *Carlisle & Jacquelin et al.,* Supreme Court No. 73-203 (1974).

Flast v. *Cohen,* 392 U.S. 83 (1968).

Guatamuz v. *Ash,* C.A. No. 155-73 (D.D.C., June 29, 1973).

Housing Authority of City and County of San Francisco v. *HUD,* 340 F. Supp. 654 (N.D. Cal. 1972).

In re Neagle, 135 U.S. 1 (1899).

Kendall v. *United States ex rel. Stokes,* 37 U.S. 524 (1838).

Kennedy v. *Sampson,* C.A. No. 1583-72 (D.D.C., Aug. 15, 1973).

Land v. *Dollar,* 330 U.S. 731 (1947).

Local 2677 A.F.G.E. v. *Phillips,* 358 F. Supp. 60 (D.D.C. 1973).

Maine v. *Fri,* No. 73-1254 (1st Cir., Nov. 2, 1973), affirming Civ. No. 14-41 (D. Me., June 29, 1973).

Marbury v. *Madison,* 5 U.S. (1 Cranch) 137 (1803).

Martin-Tricona v. *Ruckelshaus,* No. 72 C 3044 (N.D.Ill., June 29, 1973).

Minnesota v. *Fri,* no. 4-73 Civ. 133 (D. Minn., June 26, 1973).

Minnesota v. *Weinberger,* 359 F. Supp. 789 (D. Minn. 1973).

Myers v. *U.S.,* 272 U.S. 52 (1926).

Commonwealth of Pennsylvania v. *Lynn,* 362 F. Supp. 1363 (D.D.C. July 23, 1973).

Pennsylvania v. *Weinberger,* 367 F. Supp. 1378 (D.D.C. 1973).

Powell v. *McCormack,* 395 U.S. 486 (1969).

Rooney v. *Lynn,* C.A. no. 2010-73 (D.D.C. 1974).

San Francisco Redevelopment Agency v. *Nixon,* 329 F. Supp. 672 (N.D. Cal. 1971).

Snyder v. *Harris,* 394 U.S. 332 (1969).

State Highway Commission of Missouri v. *Volpe,* 479 F.2d 1099 (8th Cir. 1973).

Texas v. *Fri,* C.A. No. A-73-CA-38 (W.D. Tex., Oct. 2, 1973).

U.S. v. *Curtiss-Wright Export Corp.,* 299 U.S. 304 (1936).
U.S. v. *U.S. District Court,* 407 U.S. 297 (1972).
United States v. *Midwest Oil Co.,* 236 U.S. 459 (1915).
U.S. v. *Nixon,* 94 S.Ct. 3090 (1974).
U.S. v. *Washington Post Co.,* 403 U.S. 713 (1971).
Williams v. *Phillips,* C.A. No. 490-73 (D.D.C., June 27, 1973).
Youngstown Sheet & Tube Co. v. *Sawyer,* 343 U.S. 579 (1952).

Index